THE
ULTIMATE
RUGER
10/22

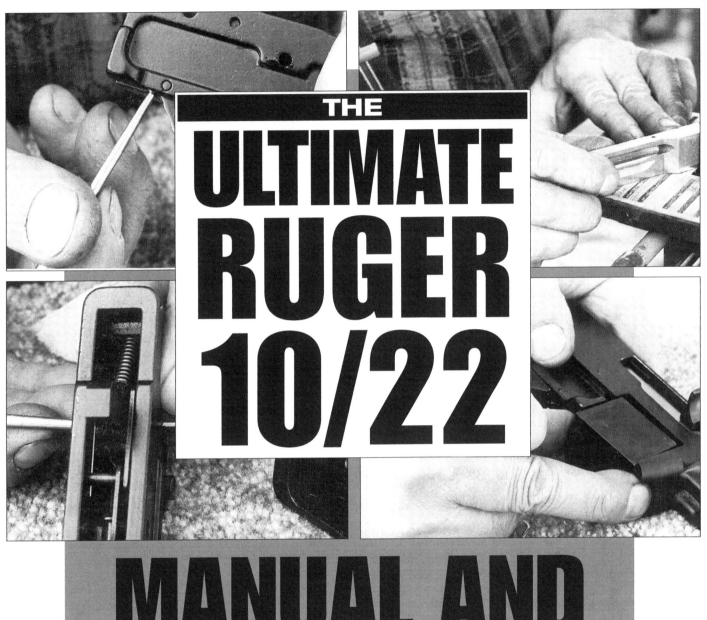

THE
ULTIMATE
RUGER
10/22

MANUAL AND
USER'S GUIDE

PALADIN PRESS • BOULDER, COLORADO

The Ultimate Ruger 10/22 Manual and User's Guide
by Mark White

Copyright © 2000 by Mark White

ISBN 13: 978-1-58160-074-2
Printed in the United States of America

Published by Paladin Press, a division of
Paladin Enterprises, Inc.
Gunbarrel Tech Center
7077 Winchester Circle
Boulder, Colorado 80301 USA
+1.303.443.7250

Direct inquiries and/or orders to the above address.

Visit our Web site at www.paladin-press.com

CONTENTS

WARNING

The manufacture, modification, possession, and use of certain firearms and suppressors are illegal without licensing from and registration with the proper authorities. It is the reader's responsibility to research and comply with all local, state, and federal laws regarding firearms. Failure to do so could result in fines and/or imprisonment.

Technical data presented here, particularly data on ammunition and on the construction, use, adjustment, and alteration of firearms, inevitably reflects the author's individual beliefs and experiences with particular firearms, equipment, and components under specific circumstances that the reader may not be able to duplicate exactly. The information in this book should therefore be used for guidance only and approached with great caution.

The author, publisher, and distributors of this book disclaim any liability from any physical damages or injuries or legal problems that a reader or user of information contained within this book may encounter. Use the material presented in this manual and any end product or by-product at your own physical and legal risk.

This book is *for academic study only.*

INTRODUCTION

This work really started in 1961 when I bought my first Ruger .22 semiautomatic target pistol. The trigger was great and the piece cycled well, but the pistol lacked that fine edge that makes a weapon really accurate. About 10 years later, I moved to Alaska and bought my first 10/22 Ruger carbine, which was very accurate. I gave it a trigger job, mounted an inexpensive 4x scope, and had a great time taking difficult shots at relatively long distances. I retired in 1990 with the idea of building sound suppressors for firearms to keep body and soul together in my declining years. I was quite surprised that my biggest sellers turned out to be suppressed systems for the Ruger 10/22 carbine and the MK II pistol.

Because of the way U.S. tax laws are interpreted, a customer avoids substantial excise tax by sending me his firearm to be suppressed, rather than having me buy the firearm and then selling the entire system to him. As a result, customers frequently send me their Ruger rifles and pistols for suppression. The modularity and sound construction of Ruger products make many of them the industry standard.

It wasn't long before it became obvious to me that these firearms could be a lot better with a little more work on their triggers, actions, and barrels. Many of my customers are gunsmiths, so when they brought me guns for suppression, we would often compare notes on ways to make things better. Some things I learned by myself, but many more ideas came from inventive interaction with friends, customers, and fellow Class II suppressor manufacturers. If I have learned anything in this life, it is that a combined pool of human brainpower is much more effective than one person working alone.

In the early 1990s I wrote two articles for *Machine Gun News* about improving the reliability and accuracy of the Ruger 10/22 rifle.

Quite a number of people wrote and called to thank me for those articles and to pass on information. On occasion I have given instructional seminars to small groups of gunsmiths who work on Ruger rimfires. I have learned so much more since writing those articles that I thought it was time for a more permanent work on the subject.

This book begins with a discussion of how to improve the 10/22 and concludes with maintenance and other problems relating to suppressed and full-auto 10/22s.

THE BASIC PARTS AND HOW THEY FUNCTION

Historically, the firearm was first developed as a crude cast-bronze bottle or tube, into which a heavy arrow or bolt was placed. The bottle was laid on the ground and discharged in the general direction of the enemy using a lit fuse or a burning brand. Not surprisingly, the likelihood of hitting a moving target with such a device was not particularly good. Soon, someone borrowed the concept of a wooden stock from the crossbow, mounted an iron tube on it, and the early musket was developed.

Now, some 500 years later, we know considerably more about what makes a firearm reliable and accurate. As we enter the 21st century, we have cased ammunition (cartridges) in a self-loading (semiautomatic) firearm, but typically our all-metal actions and barrels continue to be housed in wooden and plastic stocks. It remains to be seen if we can do better than that. Innovations come slowly, and the public is reluctant to accept anything new.

The key to understanding any firearm is to know its basic parts and how they function. Although parts and their function may differ somewhat from weapon to weapon, the basic parts are as follows.

MAGAZINE, RECEIVER, AND BARREL

The job of a magazine is to hold a number of cartridges in such a way that they may be easily released and then fed by an actuating bolt into the rear of a barrel. The function of a receiver is to hold a barrel, bolt, and magazine in proper alignment with each other so that cartridges may be properly fed, fired, and ejected. Although a magazine may be held loosely and still function reliably, a barrel must be held very securely so that it will point in exactly the same direction as each shot is fired, allowing the barrel to reach its maximum potential for accuracy.

3

STOCK

The job of the rifle stock is to act as an interface between the human shooter and the barreled action in order to allow the accurate and comfortable firing of each shot. A barreled action does not need a stock to be fired accurately—in fact, most rifles fire with far greater precision when their stocks are eliminated and a machine rest is used instead (more on this later). Most rifles need sights so that their human shooters may align and direct their bullets properly.

IRON SIGHTS

Sights for rifles come in two essential forms—iron and optical. Iron sights come standard on most Ruger rifles and pistols. The factory sights are usually adequate on the pistols, where accuracy is less of an issue and the sights are usually far enough away from one's sighting eye to allow proper focus. Because a rifle is expected to be vastly more accurate than a pistol, more is required of the 10/22 factory sighting system. The factory front sight is functional and usually effective. The factory rear sight is abominable and a waste of effort for all but the youngest, most flexible eyes. A commercial peep sight is the only acceptable alternative for those who must have an iron sight on the 10/22. The least expensive rear peep sight is made by Williams and sold by Brownells. The call number for this sight is RGRS RU22. We'll discuss optical systems in detail later.

TARGET RIFLES

Some "high-power" target shooters use the 10/22 for offhand, kneeling, and prone target practice, for those times when it is easier to get to a small-bore range or shoot off their back porch. For this, the 10/22 is fitted with a target-grade stock of fiberglass or laminated wood, a heavy target barrel up to 24 inches long, a quality front sight with variable inserts, and an easily adjustable rear sight. The trigger is tuned, and a stop is fitted to reduce overtravel. The trigger is usually set to break at 4 pounds. A two-position shooting sling is fitted.

These "high-power 10/22s" are usually accurate and fairly reliable, even with subsonic target ammunition. They are meant to simulate a military M14 or M1A1 in practice. The sights are well made and easily regulated. Curiously, these rifles are often capable of shooting more accurately with iron sights than would be possible with a scope. Good iron sights are surprisingly effective in skilled hands: light rays are apparently distorted less in open air than through the various lenses of a telescopic sight. Devotees of rifle scopes are occasionally shocked when they are beaten in a match by someone with excellent eyesight and a rifle equipped with metallic sights.

I once took three shots offhand at a rusty 1-gallon can sitting on a downed tree near a remote hunting camp in western Alaska. The rifle was a cheap, single-shot bolt-action .22, the barrel of which had been ringed and then cut off at 11 inches to get rid of the ring. The sights consisted of a cheap rear peep and a postfront made from a short piece of nail glued into a shallow hole with Marinetex. In the real world one might have been concerned about the registration of a short-barreled rifle, but the older gentleman who leased the hunting camp was not concerned with dotting i's and crossing t's. The distance was 120 yards, and my two companions chided me because the can would not fall. When we approached the object of my attention, we were all greatly surprised to see the three shots clustered in a group in the exact center of the can. The group measured less than 1/2 inch. The light had been perfect, and there was no wind. Inexpensive though it was, the rifle was described by all who hunted with it as "unusually accurate."

THE BARREL: THE HEART OF AN ACCURATE RIFLE

As the title of this chapter implies, the barrel is the core of an accurate rifle. A few factory 10/22 barrels are exceptional, but the odds are better for extreme accuracy with a factory target barrel or one of the many aftermarket match barrels currently offered. Because profile shape (exterior taper), groove and bore diameter, twist rate, chamber style, crown, and muzzle choke (or lack thereof) all affect accuracy, I will explain how barrels are made.

BARREL STEELS

When it comes to barrels, one of the first and most important choices concerns barrel material. Today there are many types of steel from which to choose, but in contrast to the automobile and truck manufacturers, makers of gun barrels don't have the industrial clout to always get the materials they want. With regard to .22 barrels, strength and longevity are rarely considered important factors. In the old days, blacksmiths pounded iron bars into long strips and then wound the strips around an iron mandrel to make a barrel. This may seem like a waste of effort today, but the blacksmiths of old knew that the strength of the metal ran with the grain, and they wanted to get as much hoop strength as possible. Today we have more automated machinery and better quality steel. Our barrel blanks are rolled out in continuous bar stock. Interestingly, the grain of the steel now stretches longitudinally, making barrel steel about 40 percent stronger lengthwise than it is in hoop strength. This is not normally a problem with a .22 LR, but when a barrel bursts it will separate into long strands, with the parting lines usually on the corners of the rifling grooves.

Even though Sporting Arms and Ammunition Manufacturers Institute (SAAMI) specifications list maximum pressures for the .22 LR as approaching 21,000 pounds per square inch (psi), the reality is that extremely thin material may be used to contain the bursting pressure of this usually mild and highly efficient round. One pistol manufacturer has successfully used a barrel liner inside a soft thermoplastic tube as a barrel. The liner in this case had a wall thickness of roughly .030 inch, equivalent to six sheets of ordinary paper. The head of a typical .22 LR cartridge is only .014 inch thick, and roughly one-third of that head is unsupported in most semiautomatic rifles and pistols. The sidewall of that same brass case is often less than .007 inch, which is just a touch thicker than a single sheet of paper. This does not mean that I am an advocate of a paper-thin barrel, but it is amazing how little material is often required to contain the pressure of a .22 LR cartridge.

The Dangers of Thin Steel Barrels

Such thin barrels will fail when a cartridge containing less than a full load of powder (or damp or oiled powder) is fired and manages to propel its bullet only partway down a barrel. The very next bullet will strike the first bullet violently, swaging them both together in a lump and swelling the barrel. In the case of a very thin barrel, this action will cause the barrel to burst, possibly injuring the person pulling the trigger.

Many people think that they can "shoot the obstruction out" of a heavy barrel by firing more rounds. What will happen instead is that more and more bullets will swage together in the bore, causing an obstruction that can only be removed by melting the lead out with a torch. Sometimes the accuracy of such a barrel is seriously impaired; sometimes it is not. One should always be on the alert for the sound of an unusual report. If an unusual sound is heard, firing should be stopped immediately and the bore should be inspected. A second shot fired into a bore obstruction always causes damage, and a wise person will always carry a cleaning rod to handle such an emergency. A solid brass or steel cleaning rod can be used to ram a single bullet out. Such a rod used to be standard in military rifles so that stuck bullets or cartridges could be removed on the spot.

Common Steels for Barrels

Given a choice, most barrel manufacturers will use a steel known in the trade as 1137 for .22

rimfire barrels. This is a soft, uniform material that is very easily machined. It is so soft that it may be cut easily with a pocket knife. In fact, on the back of my lathe I keep a small, dull knife, which I use for rounding corners and trimming burrs from this material. The 1137 steel is easily polished and takes a nice finish.

For more demanding calibers, tougher, harder steels (such as 4140 chrome-molybdenum [chrome-moly], 4130, 4150, and 4340) are used. These are a little harder to machine and rifle but hold pressure and withstand wear much more effectively. There are several stainless alloys available to barrelmakers. The chrome content makes these steels harder to cut and very abrasive; the nickel content makes them sticky. Often, stainless barrel steels will contain percentages of lead or sulfur to improve machineability, and both elements will reduce hardness and longevity to a considerable degree. The coefficient of expansion of stainless is considerably greater than regular chrome-moly steel, a factor to consider when firing multiple rounds. A few of the stainless alloys machine well, but they all cost more and can be difficult to work. Those who want a stainless barrel can expect to pay from 10 to 40 percent more for 416 stainless (the most common alloy) than for other steels. Typically, if you live on or near the ocean or in a hot, humid climate, the stainless alloys are worth the money. Otherwise they are not. Stainless is a much more difficult material to machine into an accurate barrel. A few of the factory stainless barrels I've seen were accurate, but most were not.

BARREL DRILLING

Barrel material is purchased in bar form and cut to length on automatic saws. Typical lengths for the 10/22 are 16, 18, and 22 inches. Most aftermarket barrels for the 10/22 start out about 1 inch in diameter and finish at .920 inch. These blanks are cut a little long and then sent to an automatic deep-hole drilling machine for boring.

The deep-hole drill is unusual in that it has only one cutting edge. As might be expected, it is quite long. It has a tiny hole down the center of its shank, through which cutting oil is forced under pressure. The oil exits near the drill's tip, where it picks up waste metal (or swarf), washing it down a groove milled alongside the shank and out the drilled end of the barrel-to-be.

As one might imagine, the barrel business has been around for quite some time, and the machines that do this work are very specialized. Those who run them have amassed a considerable amount of knowledge related to boring, reaming, and rifling. All barrelmakers love the free machining qualities of 1137. They use it whenever possible, even though it ultimately wears more rapidly than some other alloys. It takes about 13 minutes to drill a 10/22 barrel on an automatic machine. Factory barrel production for the 10/22 runs from 12,000 to 20,000 units per month.

REAMING AND TWIST RATES

After being drilled each barrel then proceeds to the next stage, where the bore is reamed to final size (from .211 to .218 inch) prior to being rifled. One can measure a number of different .22 bullets, finding them to be from .223 (rare) to .224, .225, and .226 inch in diameter. The best accuracy will result when the lead bullet is ever so slightly larger than the groove diameter of the barrel—one- or two-tenths of a thousandth of an inch would be about right. The lead bullets in .22 LR ammo are extremely soft and will easily extrude into much smaller barrels. Many rifling lands are from two- to five-thousandths of an inch in height.

The rifling process will either cut or press the grooves into the bore. Different twists are used in an attempt to make the twist just fast enough to stabilize the bullet. I tend to like bores that are a little tight and twists that are faster than normal so as to stabilize bullets under a variety of wind and weather conditions. I like the minor diameter of the bore (from land to land) to be from .211 to .215 inch, with the major diameter (groove to groove) from .222 to .223 inch. I like a twist rate from one turn in 12 inches to one turn in 14

inches. Many bores I have examined are .216 x .224 inch, with a twist rate of one turn in 16 inches. This may work well in warm climates, but in colder, denser air such a twist may leave a bullet unstable. When the .223 cartridge was developed for a military rifle it was found to be accurate enough in a warm climate, but when the round was tested in the subzero climate of Alaska, it would not stay on a dinner plate at 25 yards.

BULLET STABILITY

The little .223 bullet was designed to be unstable, tumbling after hitting its target. The .22 LR bullet is of soft lead and has no such limitations. I feel that superb stability is important for this little round to remain accurate under all conditions.

RIFLING

There are three potential rifling processes that may be used to rifle .22 LR barrels: broach, button, and cut.

Broach Rifling

A broach is fairly long, difficult to make, expensive, and fragile. It has cutting teeth that are smaller near the front and progressively larger toward the rear. As a broach is pulled through a reamed bore, each tooth takes a progressively deeper bite out of the bottom of each spiral groove. Broaches are very hard to sharpen and maintain and are said to make very accurate barrels, since they cut the rifling rather than shape it under pressure. They are often used on high-end pistol barrels, where they do their work rapidly and effectively, but they are rarely used on rifle barrels, since the gullets between the teeth tend to rapidly plug up with metal shavings on a long pull—with disastrous consequences for both broach and barrel. Broached rifling is similar to cut rifling in that it does not build stress or pressure into the barrel's metal. Many .22 rifle barrels were broached 30 to 50 years ago, but almost no barrels are rifled using this technique today.

Button Rifling

Button rifling employs a small carbide button (with an impression of the rifling grooves and twist) that is drawn through a reamed and lubricated bore. The buttons last fairly well and are cheap to produce in contrast to a broach. Aside from hooking up the draw rod, the process takes from three to ten seconds to complete. The draw rod is twisted at the same rate as the button to discourage a skip or slip in the twist rate, which has been known to occur.

As a button passes through a reamed hole, it forces the barrel metal to extrude or flow around its impression of the rifling grooves. It is imperative that the outside of the barrel be uniform and parallel (not tapered), or else the button will cause the barrel to stretch in thin areas temporarily and the button to dig in deeper in thicker areas. Great stress is built into the barrel walls during this rifling process. When the blank is turned to size and contour, that stress is relieved, causing the bore to be largest where the wall is thinnest (at the muzzle).

A friend and I were talking about this recently, and I performed a quick experiment on the lathe to illustrate the situation. I took a short chunk of .22 barrel blank that was about 7/8 inch in diameter. I measured the groove diameter of the bore with a set of digital calipers, coming up with .2231 inch. After I turned a short section to 5/8-inch outside diameter (OD), I remeasured the same area of the bore, coming up with .2243 inch. The bore had expanded a little over 1/1,000 of an inch when only 1/8 inch of metal was removed from its exterior.

I then took another short section and ground six parallel grooves with an abrasive blade held in a 14-inch chop saw to simulate fluting. Again, the bore expanded a little over 1/1,000 of an inch. This "reverse choke" or mild blunderbuss effect at the muzzle of many rifles and pistols does not encourage extreme accuracy. It has been proven that a soft lead bullet wears easily during its trip down a rifled bore. A slight choke of from 1/2 to 1/1000 of an inch right at the muzzle will help compensate for wear, thus providing the departing bullet with better direction at the last moment of departure. Now you know why barrels made for target work on the 10/22 rifle and MK II pistol are just as thick at the muzzle as they are at the breech. An even better situation would result if these target barrels were 1/8 inch larger in outside diameter at the muzzle, since that might induce the .0005-inch muzzle choke deemed desirable.

Cut Rifling

Cut rifling is made using a single tooth to cut all of the grooves separately, which requires a great number of passes. First, the barrel blank is drilled and reamed. The reamed hole will be the minor diameter (land diameter) of the rifled bore. The barrel is then set in a fixture, and the single tooth is drawn by its tiny rod down its spiral path and then returned to battery. On the next pass it is rotated 1/6 of a turn (for six grooves) and drawn down the barrel. If the barrel were to have two, three, four, five, seven, or eight grooves, the tooth would be rotated the appropriate amount. On each pass it cuts a mere 1/10,000 inch of material from the bottom of one groove. After going around the barrel once, the cutter is advanced another tenth, and the process begins anew.

It can take up to four hours to cut-rifle one barrel, although one hour would be about right for a short .22 LR barrel. Compared with the 10 seconds it takes to button-rifle a barrel, it is clear that this process requires an inordinate amount of time. This is especially so if large quantities of barrels need to be produced.

Because each stroke cuts rather than swages material, a cut-rifled barrel tends to have the least amount of stress induced in its bore. If a broach gets bent, if a button runs into material that is harder on one side than the other, or if the button was soldered a little crooked onto its draw rod, then the grooves will be deeper on one side than the other. A small thing, perhaps, and hard to measure on the completed product, but the end result will be a barrel that lacks extreme precision. If hundreds of thousands of barrels per month are turned out, they will not all be extremely accurate. A cut-rifled bore, if done properly, can have a land diameter that is most uniform and grooves that are precisely the same depth. Although a button-rifled barrel may be accurate, a cut-rifled bore has the best potential for extreme accuracy.

Barrelmaker Cliff LaBounty tells an amusing story. A few years ago, Smith & Wesson's Custom Shop contracted with him to cut-rifle a handful of .22 barrel blanks for one of its target pistol models. Cliff did this and sent the barrels to S&W. A short time later he got a nastygram from the shop saying that the barrels did not meet specifications and would be rejected. Interestingly, Cliff later found one of the rifled blanks lying near one of his machines and gave the blank to Mike Curtis, a Marine Corps armorer at Quantico. Mike worked the blank into a completed barrel that he fitted into a target pistol, which he in turn gave to shooter Mario Lazoya. Mario used the pistol to win the Quantico Regional, scoring 100-10x and becoming the 1992 World Champion in the process. Cliff has the winning target hanging in his shop to this day. He photocopied the target and sent a copy to the S&W Custom Shop, but received no reply.

A WARNING ON BLOOP TUBES

Bloop tubes are sections of steel or plastic pipe that have been slipped over and attached to the muzzle of a target rifle. The reason bloop tubes are used is ostensibly to increase the distance between the front and rear sight. On a rifle, this typically results in a sight radius of between 40 and 50 inches in length. On a pistol, it would be from 20 to 24 inches.

Bloop tubes are so named because they change the "crack" of a .22's muzzle report to something more resembling a "bloop." Bloop tubes significantly reduce the intensity of the report, some by as much as 11 decibels. BATF has held that any muzzle device that reduces the intensity of a muzzle report by more than two or three decibels will fit the legal definition of a silencer and

has prosecuted at least one case where unregistered devices were either used or possessed.

Many who use these devices feel that because their tubes are of plastic or because steel tubes are held on by temporary means (such as with a set screw or duct tape), they are not really silencers in the legal sense. Nothing could be further from the truth. Bloop tubers should be warned that the materials and methods of attachment will have absolutely no bearing on whether a muzzle device is legally construed to be a silencer. In fact, you would be on much firmer legal ground if a steel tube was actually welded to a barrel, especially if that tube went all the way to the receiver. In the past BATF has not made a serious effort to prosecute those who own or use bloop tubes. However, as we all know, this policy could change in the twinkling of an eye. In fact, as this book is being edited, the policy has changed, and owners of bloop tubes are being prosecuted.

BARREL LENGTH

There is much controversy over how long a .22 LR barrel should be. Many feel that because the accurate muzzle-loading Kentucky long rifles of the late 1700s and early 1800s had long barrels, all rifles should have long barrels to be accurate. Because we were taught this concept as youngsters, it is rooted deeply in our minds—but the main reason for long barrels on the Kentucky rifles was that the crude gunpowder of the day needed that length for an efficient burn.

In reality, a shorter barrel is inherently stiffer and vibrates less, so shorter barrels should be considered for greater accuracy. In turning rifle barrels on a lathe, I quickly discovered that a moderate decrease in length will lead to a drastic reduction in vibration and tool chatter. I have whacked quite a number of 18 1/2-inch factory 10/22 barrels to 16 1/4 inches and have noted a significant increase in accuracy. In terms of velocity, it may be that we get the best return out of an investment when using a 16-inch barrel. Note the two accompanying charts that bear the results of three barrel-chopping experiments Al

Paulson and I conducted in the springs of 1995 and 2000. We used a variety of ammunition, which was intended to be a fair sampling of the hundreds of varieties of .22 ammo currently offered in the United States.

The first thing an astute observer will note is that 10/22 barrels are about 70 feet per second (fps) *slower* than 77/22 barrels. This is because the 77/22 barrel has a tighter chamber, which engages each bullet into the rifling as a cartridge is chambered. The tight chamber causes each bullet to stay in its cartridge a little longer before being forced forward by the expanding gas. This raises chamber pressure somewhat, resulting in a more complete powder burn. (It is a little known fact that efficient cartridges force most of the burning to take place within the case.) Once a bullet begins to move down the barrel, temperatures quickly cool and pressures drop like a rock. Since bullet acceleration is directly related to pressure on the base, it can be seen that the first 30 percent of the barrel is doing most of the work. In terms of velocity, a 12-inch barrel is usually as fast as a 24-inch barrel. I found it interesting that both barrel types (10/22 and 77/22) typically produced their highest velocities, across the board, at 16 inches.

Accuracy from a short barrel should be better. It was about 20 years ago that I spent several days playing with that Alaskan camp rifle with its 11-inch barrel, and it was among the most accurate firearms I've ever shot. Within reason, a shorter barrel should be more accurate because vibration and barrel whip will be less. Also, the time that a bullet spends traveling down its barrel will be greatly reduced. (I do not believe, however, that a 2-inch barrel will be as accurate as one 12 to 16 inches long.) Those in the civilian world are normally limited to a 16-inch barrel on a rifle. They may own a shorter rifle, but most have to pay a $200 transfer tax to BATF to possess one legally. Al Paulson and I are both federally licensed Class II Manufacturers, and we used registered short-barreled rifles for our barrel-chopping experiments.

Let's talk briefly about why the semiautomatic 10/22's chamber cannot be as tight as that of a bolt-action rifle. A bolt gun is slowly operated by an external force. It usually has two extractors and a powerful camming action to assist in removing a spent case or a dud cartridge. The 10/22 gets its only operating impulse from the brief rearward push of the cartridge *after* the pressure has dropped substantially. During the *peak* of the pressure curve, the cartridge walls stick to the chamber walls, delaying rearward movement. I have firelapped hundreds of .22 barrels, using nothing more than a 1-pound hammer, safety glasses, and a gloved left hand. Rarely does a shell eject on its own.

10/22 — .22LR VELOCITY VS. BARREL LENGTH
(Measured in Feet Per Second)

Barrel Length in Inches	CCI Stinger	Rem. Viper	Win. Wildcat	Rem. HiVel	Rem. StVel	Baikal JrBrs	Average	Maximum Velocity
18.5	1,536	1,318	1,229	1,190	1,094	973	1,223	-1%
16	1,539	1,323	1,226	1,194	1,118	983	1,231	
14	1,531	1,328	1,212	1,179	1,119	960	1,222	-1%
12	1,502	1,307	1,197	1,167	1,083	937	1,199	-3%
10	1,464	1,287	1,175	1,149	1,076	934	1,179	-4%
8	1,441	1,252	1,152	1,104	1,060	922	1,155	-7%
6	1,374	1,201	1,088	1,042	1,000	870	1,096	-11%
4	1,236	1,054	1,004	1,021	931	785	1,005	-18%
2	948	820	794	792	720	608	780	-37%

(Chart provided by Sound Technology, P.O. Box 391, Pelham, AL 35124.)

THE BARREL: THE HEART OF AN ACCURATE RIFLE

77/22 .22LR VELOCITY VS. BARREL LENGTH

Barrel Length	CCI Stinger	Rem. Viper	Rem. Hi Vel.	Rem. S. Vel.	Aguila SSS
28	1,532	1,308	1,213	1,095	649
26	1,541	1,316	1,225	1,107	682
24	1,549	1,324	1,236	1,119	721
22	1,557	1,332	1,245	1,129	755
20	1,565	1,340	1,254	1,138	796
18	1,573	1,348	1,263	1,149	821
16	1,581	1,356	1,274	1,157	841
14	1,570	1,342	1,264	1,149	865
12	1,536	1,321	1,243	1,143	894
10	1,514	1,283	1,230	1,138	908
8	1,486	1,247	1,209	1,115	896
6	1,421	1,224	1,173	1,095	834
4	1,310	1,121	1,054	1,027	732
2	1,078	960	904	850	561

RELIABLE CYCLING AND CHAMBERS

Because the 10/22 has only a single extractor and a tiny operating handle, its chamber must be long and loose. If a dud cartridge fails to ignite in the field, and if its bullet has already been engraved into the rifling in a tight chamber, extracting that cartridge will leave the bullet stuck in the bore. The rifle will be tied up and quite useless without a proper cleaning rod to remove the stuck bullet. A long, sloppy chamber will prevent that from happening. Much effort has been spent in developing a tapered, funnel-shaped chamber that will allow free and easy insertion and extraction yet still be accurate. The Bentz chamber reamer, as sold by Brownells, comes closest to providing the optimal mix of performance characteristics.

Some use a match chamber, but this generates both chambering and extraction difficulties. There is little in life more frustrating than a semiautomatic rifle in the field that fails to function. A nylon chamber brush powered with a short, bent rod will allow chamber cleaning through the ejection port.

Another trick used extensively on the M1 rifle, M1 carbine, and the Thompson .45 submachine gun during World War II when these weapons cycled unreliably was to coat the first cartridge in a magazine with a heavy oil. I have used this on both the 10/22 carbine and the MK II pistol with dramatic results. One should use a heavy oil with a high lubricity. I use chainsaw bar and chain oil, or 90-weight gear lube. One drop on the tip of the first bullet in the magazine just before firing will coat the chamber for 20 to 30 rounds. Do not use a thin penetrating oil like WD-40 or Break Free, which may quickly get into the cartridge and ruin the priming mixture or, worse, contaminate the powder charge just enough to get a bullet stuck halfway down the bore.

It should also be mentioned that in the 10/22 carbine, clearing a jam is much easier if you reach through the magazine well (instead of the smaller ejection port) with a dull knife or a small screwdriver. As always, protect your eyes with polycarbonate (Lexan) shooting glasses or safety glasses. I've not yet had a shell discharge while clearing a jam, but it would not be a pretty sight without eye protection. I never do anything like this without shooting glasses.

For us older members of society, Dillion Precision sells shooting glasses with a little magnifier at the bottom of each lens. These glasses have been tested to withstand a load of birdshot from about 40 yards away. I trust them.

FIRELAPPING

The old-time barrelmakers spent many an hour hunched over a barrel vise with an abrasive-charged bore lap. One who is practiced can run a cleaning patch down a bore and feel tight spots. Barrels are almost never lapped these days, and very few shooters know what the inside of their barrel looks or feels like.

The leade or forcing cone or throat of a new barrel has lands with rough, sharp corners. A soft lead bullet will not take rifling uniformly over these corners. Every new barrel or newly chambered barrel should have these areas deburred. Firelapping is the only method that can do this properly and effectively. In the past I have purchased 800-grit silicon carbide paste from Brownells to do this work. NECO now offers graded abrasives of very high quality for this. Brownells also carries NECO's firelapping manual and kit. Because I do quite a number of barrels, my procedure varies from that in NECO's manual.

I take out 40 cartridges of the lowest velocity I can find. I use standard-velocity .22 LR target ammo or, better yet, Federal or CCI CB Long ammo. NECO's kit contains various grades of abrasive, but I only use 800- and 1,200-grit silicon carbide. Included in NECO's kit are two small steel bars or plates. I put a small dab of the 1,200-grit abrasive paste on one plate and roll each bullet between it and the other plate, impregnating the cylindrical portion of 10 lead bullets with the abrasive. I then put a dab of the 800-grit paste on the same plate and roll that abrasive into another 10 bullets. The lower numbered abrasive is of a coarser grit and cuts more aggressively. I fire the 800-grit bullets first, followed by the 10 bullets impregnated with 1,200-grit paste.

I then take the gun apart and run cleaning patches from the chamber end down the bore and out the muzzle. I remove the patch and withdraw the rod. All 10/22s I work on have a cleaning hole bored in the rear of the receiver to allow easy cleaning from the rear. If yours is not so modified, the barrel will have to be removed, which is easily accomplished with an Allen wrench. I am very careful about the barrel's muzzle. I never clean any firearm from its muzzle. To do so would surely damage the crown, and the crown at the muzzle is probably the most important area of an accurate barrel.

While running patches through I carefully feel for roughness, paying special attention to the throat or leade of the chamber. After four or five patches I carefully examine the leade through a strong hand lens in full sunlight. My shop has a row of south-facing windows, and I see better from the unlit shop while looking at the chamber area in the light from the windows. If the leade area needs more metal removed, I will prepare another five bullets rolled in 1,200-grit paste and fire them.

Having the barrel out of the action eases the process greatly. A bore scope is a useful tool here, but at $1,400 each, they are impractical for most. A friend picked up a used and discarded cystoscope from a urologist, and I sometimes borrow this if there is an area inside the bore that I want to examine thoroughly. As long as the bore has no constrictions smaller than the muzzle, the only two areas that make any difference are the leade of the chamber and the last inch or so near the crown.

The middle of the bore can be pitted and dark, but if the throat and muzzle are perfect, that barrel will shoot with extreme accuracy. If the middle of the barrel is perfect and the throat is belled out or the crown worn or damaged, the barrel will not shoot accurately. I have an old 8mm Mauser rifle that lay under a tank on a battlefield in France for two years. Its barrel is deeply pitted, yet it will shoot a 2-inch group at 400 yards with iron sights. Again, the middle means little—the ends are everything.

FINAL POLISH

The final sequence in firelapping is very important, yet often ignored. When the last 20 of my cartridges are fired, they are charged with J.B. Bore Cleaning Paste, which is also available through Brownells. This last is a medium-weight grease filled with an unusually fine abrasive and polishing powder. I don't know what the makeup of the material is—I don't want to know. I only know that it delivers a polish to the bore beyond any I have been able to achieve by any other method.

I use the small end of a cut-down tongue depressor or Popsicle stick and apply a small dab of JB paste about equal to half of the volume of a lead .22 bullet. I push the material directly into the chamber, insert a cartridge, and fire. This sequence is repeated 20 times. There will be those who say that this dab of grease constitutes a bore obstruction and could ring or bulge the barrel. And so it could if it were placed at the muzzle—as could a dab of mud, a section filled with ice, or a large insect. Insects are a big problem in the South, so I usually check the bore before firing any firearm. However, if the polishing compound is placed in the chamber, it will surround and move out with the bullet, starting out at zero velocity.

After the application of bore paste, the barrel is again cleaned from the rear using only a 3/16-inch cleaning rod and 7/8-inch cotton patches. After three or four are used, these patches will start coming out clean. If you remember the force required to run a patch through before firelapping, then you will be very pleased with the ease and smoothness of the bore after firelapping. The bore will stay fairly clean because the polished surface doesn't provide much for fouling to cling to.

STRAIGHTNESS AND CONCENTRICITY

I had a friend who taught pottery at a large university. When he would form a clay pot on a wheel in front of a class, he would frequently cut it down the middle with a wire so the class members could view the cross section. We rarely do this with barrels, but it would be an educational exercise. I have cut barrels in two on a number of occasions, using only the rear section. It is amazing how few of them have their bores in the exact center—fewer than 1 percent. Even in shortening a factory barrel from 20 to 16 inches, that same figure of 1 percent holds true. Does this do much harm? Probably not. But continuous firing will heat up the thinner section more rapidly, expanding and walking the shots away from the thinner area. This is not a big deal at 10 feet but is very noticeable at 100 yards.

One might expect a lack of concentricity in an inexpensive factory barrel, but how about a very expensive, select, air-gauged, match-grade barrel? Same thing, sometimes worse. I have cut very expensive, match-grade rifle barrels into pieces varying from 4 to 11 inches to make pistol barrels. Sometimes the bore was 5/16 inch from the center, where it should have been. When I mentioned this to barrelmaker LaBounty, he was not surprised. He said very few bores are truly straight.

Aside from cutting a barrel in two, there are ways one can tell how straight a bore is. A practiced eye can look down a barrel in good light and get an idea how bad it is by rotating it and looking for the differences. Centerless ground gauge pins are available in any diameter. These are about 3 or 4 inches long, straight, hardened, very parallel, and come in increments of .0001 inch. If your minor bore diameter was .2111 inch, you could procure a gauge pin .2110 inch in diameter. Assuming no bore constrictions (ha!) when pushing this pin through a clean bore, curved areas would be tight because the straight pin would bind in the curved portion. A soft pin would gall and stick, but a hardened pin would not. It can usually be driven out from the other end if (when) it gets stuck. This is probably the best method of determining the straightness of a bore.

Fifty to 100 years ago, barrel shops were full of wizened old men armed with barrel-straightening presses, which were large wheel/screw devices placed above head height, with a light source. It took years of experience to use these well, and the old men were very good at what they did. No one does this anymore, and that saddens me. Apparently the world has discovered that for single-aimed shots the only things that matter are the throat and the crown. For rapid-fire, high-power shooting, a straight, concentric bore continues to be important.

THE TENSIONED BARREL

The tensioned barrel is a system designed to provide stiffness and stability without excessive weight. I developed this system about 20 years ago for larger caliber rifles. It involves a steel sleeve or tube that is slid over the outside of a barrel. The muzzle is threaded, and a nut is used to pull the barrel in permanent tension, while the tube is held in compression. This can be likened to a piece of string (the barrel) pulled straight inside a cardboard tube (the sleeve). In an extreme situation the barrel can be quite slender, with the walls of the tube just thick enough to support the compression forces. This provides great stiffness without excessive weight. With the 10/22 barrel I use a 9/16-inch nut pulling against a 4130 steel tube with a wall thickness of .049 inch and an OD of 7/8 inch.

When first setting up such a system, turn the nut with a torque wrench in ever-advancing increments, while shooting groups off a bench rest. This system is especially useful when trying to tune a barrel to a specific brand and lot of factory ammunition, at the temperature where the most use is expected. Typically, the groups will get smaller and smaller as the nut is tightened. When the groups start to open up again, you know you've gone too far. You should then back off to the setting where the tightest group or "sweetest spot" was found. If the sleeve is of the same steel alloy as the barrel, the expansion/contraction coefficients will be the same. This system is very tolerant of temperature variations, typically shooting to the same point of impact whether hot or cold. After I wrote about tensioned barrels in two gun magazines, a few aftermarket manufacturers took the concept and began to sell lightweight, tensioned barrel systems. They usually use 6061 T6 aluminum or carbon fiber for the sleeve.

It should be mentioned that it is possible to

introduce a bit of choke to the muzzle area by tightening the nut, because pressure on the threads will cause the bore to constrict. For this reason, the length of the tube should cause the nut to cover all of the threads at the muzzle. Because an opening barrel after a choke will lessen accuracy, it would not do to have an inch of threads exposed.

BARREL WEAR

The two most commonly used steels for barrels appear to be 1137 and 4140, although there are many alloys that can be used to provide good service.

I once thought that barrel wear would not be a problem but then began to examine some of the used 10/22s coming in for repair. Surprisingly, the action will function effectively for between 300,000 and 500,000 rounds. By then it will be tired and loose, but it will still function. A good barrel made of 1137 will remain accurate through 60,000 rounds, at which point it will begin to lose its edge. It will be fairly accurate for another 10,000 rounds, but by then its throat will be enlarged and eccentric. Some rifles can be turned 180 degrees in their socket, set back an inch or so, rechambered and recrowned, and shoot well for another 50,000 rounds. The 10/22 is not one of these, since its claw and socket do not allow for this. If you are lucky your barrel will be made of 4140 instead of 1137. A barrel made of 4140 should be good for upward of 100,000 rounds before its throat gets tired. Barrels will wear faster if they are used in machine guns or if shot a lot in hot weather.

So how, one wonders, do people get so many rounds through a barrel? When I was a kid I had a bolt-action .22. Money was hard to come by, and I hoarded my ammunition. I shot every day but only expended a few well-aimed rounds at a time. Things have changed. Today, many will buy four to ten bricks (500 rounds per brick) of ammo before heading out to a range or a favorite woodlot. They'll bring a number of magazines and a couple of magazine loaders to make things easier on their fingers. Two men and their wives, sons, and daughters will easily go through five or six bricks in an hour. The 10/22 is one of the few rifles that can take this kind of punishment week after week.

Some people wonder why the soft, lead, well-lubricated .22 LR round eventually wears out the throat in the barrel. The main answer comes in two words: ground glass. The priming mixture contains ground borosilicate glass. This is not a minor component but an important ingredient, since the fine-glass particles aid the ignition process when the priming ring is struck and crushed by the firing pin. Borosilicate glass (often used in cooking wear) is much harder and sharper than the greenish soda-lime glass we see used in such things as windows. With each shot a fine layer of the hard, sharp glass particles is distributed throughout the chamber and bore. As each lead bullet enters the throat, it becomes permeated with this abrasive and, bit by bit, takes a little metal out with each shot. The heat of the expanding gas also takes a toll, briefly hardening microscopic grains of metal in the throat. In large-bore firearms, this is a major force in the deterioration process. In the .22 LR, it is less so.

Because of gravity, more of the powdered glass lies in the bottom of the barrel, with the result that the side of the throat nearest the earth is eroded more rapidly. More of the lower side of the barrel is similarly worn, but the bore is not nearly so affected as the throat. The very edge of the crown is similarly worn by glass particles blown by rapidly moving gasses, but this wear tends to be fairly uniform and may be easily touched up on a lathe. After 60,000 to 100,000 rounds, the bullets are being forced into the lands in a crooked or skewed fashion because the bottom of the throat has been egged out. You can usually tell how used a barrel is by how deeply the rear face of the barrel has been eroded: the bolt beats a mixture of bullet lube and ground glass against this face. When the impression of the bolt is about .025-inch deep in the rear face, it is time to toss that barrel. New blued barrels from Ruger are only about $40. A bargain! Stainless barrels approach $80. New aftermarket match barrels

start at $90 and go up to $500. The intelligent design and modularity of the 10/22 allow a barrel change in less than five minutes.

SPOT HARDENING

The bolt block in the 10/22 is made of high-quality, hardened steel. On the forward stroke that bolt chambers a round and then slams into the barrel. After the last round has been fired and ejected, the bolt slams into the barrel again, this time without the cushioning effect of a chambering shell. In the early development stage (before sales occurred), Ruger had some serious problems with the bolt deforming the rear of the barrel, collapsing the upper rear of the chamber. The short-term home remedy was to remove the barrel and open the chamber up again with a short piece of chainsaw file or a small burr in a Dremel tool. The long-term Ruger cure was to spot-harden the rear face of each barrel with an acetylene torch or an induction coil. This has worked very well and totally cured the problem.

When you take a stainless barrel out of a 10/22 action it is usually possible to see some color left over from the heat-treating process. Of course, this color is covered by blueing in blued barrels. Some aftermarket barrels are now being sold without the rear face being hardened, and I predict that these will have problems, so don't throw away your chainsaw file. It is easy to tell whether a barrel's rear face has been hardened. Try a little corner of the rear face with a file: it is usually so hard that a file won't touch it.

HEAT TREATING

Few bother to heat-treat an entire .22 rimfire barrel any more, and this is a shame. The life and rigidity of a barrel could be greatly enhanced with a proper heat treatment. Simply stated, with conventional high-carbon steels, the metal is brought close to red heat (about 1,000°F) and then plunged into an oil or saltwater bath to quickly cool and freeze the metal structure. This makes it very hard and as brittle as glass. The same metal is then loaded into a furnace, where it is slowly brought up to between 400 and 700°F. At the specified temperature (which is of course different for various alloys and a specific hardness), the furnace is turned off and the pieces are allowed to cool slowly over a period of hours or days. This second heat treatment draws the metal, allowing it to have a certain hardness and resistance to abrasion, yet still have a measure of toughness and ductility. Glass-hard barrel steel would be brittle and dangerous. Dead-soft steel will wear quickly. Properly hardened, heat-treated barrels will be stiffer and should last two to three times as long as conventional untreated barrels.

The only .22 rifle I currently have in my battery with a heat-treated barrel is a Chinese copy of a BRNO, bolt-action, five-shot military trainer. I paid $90 for it new in 1988. Unfortunately, this model is no longer imported into the United States. Its barrel is quite hard and very stiff. I know, because I cut it from 23 inches down to 16 inches and recrowned it. It may be ugly, but it is the most accurate .22 rifle I have ever owned.

Manufacturers don't like to mess with heat treating because it adds time and an extra two steps. In terms of production, manufacturers prefer steel that is dead soft and easy to machine. We currently have a number of different steel alloys that use various hardening procedures. Most but not all use the old heat/quench/heat/draw procedure.

MELONITING

Meloniting is a process that infuses a proprietary salt into the surface of iron or steel. In this process, a barrel is lowered into a bath of molten salt at roughly 1,600°F. It is moved back and forth or up and down in that bath, so that the salt is encouraged to flow through the bore, entering and bonding with all surfaces. When the reaction is complete the very hot barrel is removed and allowed to cool. The process adds about .0003 inch to all surfaces of the barrel, rendering them very hard and quite tough.

My best guess is that a Melonited .22 barrel would last at least three times longer than an untreated barrel. All Glock pistol barrels and slides are treated with a similar process that has a different, European name. This process is fairly expensive for individual units but might be reasonable if large-scale barrelmakers decided to integrate the process into their system. If you decide to have this done, make sure that the barrel you send is accurate and sound in every other way. Remember that this process will add .0003 inch to all surfaces. Your bore and chamber will thus shrink by .0006 inch. Further work is usually not done on a Melonited barrel because it is too hard to work with normal cutting tools. You must be careful when handling a barrel heated to 1,600°F. It is very soft at that temperature and could easily sag. I do not know how the rear surface of a Melonited barrel will stand up to the battering from the bolt.

CRYOGENIC TREATMENT

Most barrels have a certain amount of internal tension, but there is a feeling among the benchrest crowd that cryogenic treatment enhances barrel accuracy. An owner typically sends his barrel off to a cryo shop, where the barrel is placed in a chamber and cooled to roughly -320°F. The barrel is then slowly brought up to 300°F and then back to room temperature. The metal is said to then have greater wear resistance, and the barrel is typically more accurate. The lowest charge for this treatment I have seen is $35, but you might get it done cheaper for a 10/22 because its barrel is so much smaller than most.

This treatment may sound strange, but it typically results in better accuracy. For a new barrel without any major flaws, firelapping and cryo treatment will both result in an increase in accuracy. For a tensioned barrel, which is already more resistant to vibration and flutter, there is usually no additional increase in accuracy with cryo treatment.

CUTTING A TAPERED BARREL TO LENGTH

Barrels that are straight (i.e., not tapered) may be cut to length easily with either a hacksaw or an abrasive chopsaw. They may then be faced off at the muzzle and given a crown on a lathe or with a piloted cutter.

Tapered barrels are much more difficult to cut properly. I will describe the process I use to trim a barrel back to 16 1/4 inches on a lathe.

The parallel shank of the rear of the barrel is held in an accurate, three-jawed chuck. Both of my lathes have accurate chucks, with less than .0005 inch of true indicated runout. The muzzle of the barrel is fitted to a live center in the tailstock. The lathe is turned on, and a small triangular bit is used to circumscribe a deep groove around the area where the barrel is to be cut. I leave the lathe running and use a hacksaw with a touch of cutting oil to finish the cut. When it reaches the bore, the hacksaw blade

jumps a little. At this point I stop the lathe and carefully finish the cut by hand. Once the muzzle section has been removed, I turn the lathe back on and carefully file the muzzle smooth. I then lightly deburr the sharp edge of the bore with a small, sharp knife.

The live center in the tailstock is advanced to support the new muzzle while I reposition the barrel, holding the shank lightly with a very small portion (1/8 inch) of the chuck's jaws. Few barrels are truly straight and parallel, and I do not want to telegraph any axial misalignment of the shank into the barrel's muzzle. I tighten the chuck just enough to hold the barrel securely. A new, sharp center drill with an aggressive rake is set into the tailstock. It is important that the smaller portion of the drill be less than the bore diameter. I usually choose a center drill with its center portion about 1/8 inch in diameter and an outer diameter of at least 3/8 inch. The center drill is carefully advanced into the muzzle of the barrel.

The gearing of the lathe is disconnected. I then turn the headstock of the lathe with my left hand, while slowly advancing the drill held in the tailstock with my right hand. A considerable amount of "feel" is used to get a clean, symmetrical cut (an operation this sensitive requires a few drops of cutting oil). The last advance is made in an increment of .001 to .002 inch, followed by a single, complete revolution. Unorthodox as it may seem, I've performed this operation hundreds of times, and it has always produced extremely accurate barrels. The center drill pulls evenly into the material if the muzzle is truly square and if the bit has been ground properly with symmetrical cutting edges. Turning the lathe by hand is the only way I would attempt to perform this operation. Trying to do this under power will cause chatter and ruin the crown.

I have also used a 60-degree, piloted counterbore (as produced by Clymer and sold by Brownells) in an electric drill with equally effective results. Some feel that the piloted counterbore is the only way to countersink a barrel, their point being that few barrels are perfectly straight and that it is therefore impossible to do a perfect job with a bore that wobbles imperfectly in a lathe. This point is valid. You might think that a rotating pilot will damage the bore. However, if the pilot is properly sized, polished, and lubricated, it probably will not damage the bore. You must pay particular attention to alignment when driving the piloted counterbore. Pulling it off to one side while it is cutting could damage the bore or crown. Turning the tool by hand will dull it very rapidly; I think this is because the user inadvertently turns the tool backward at the end of each stroke or causes uneven pressure to be applied. I know that the quickest way to ruin a counterbore is to lend it to someone who will use it by hand.

A Q-tip or cotton swab may be used to check to see that no burrs exist at the muzzle. If burrs do exist, the fibers of the swab will snag on them. Burrs can be either felt or observed under a strong hand lens.

The 60-degree countersink serves a dual purpose: it leaves the end of the muzzle at the point where a live or rotating center in the tailstock may be used to turn the barrel, and it provides a finished crown. You might think that the live center would damage the crown in some way, but I have not found this to be so. I am very careful with my live center and would replace it if it began to be untrue. Many who are interested in extreme accuracy opt for either a flat crown (90 degrees to the axis of the bore) or an 11-degree crown.

It may not matter what the angle of the muzzle crown is, as long as it remains symmetrical. I like the 60-degree (included angle) crown because I can replace the barrel in the lathe at any time and again use a live center in the tailstock to hold that end as I turn and work on the barrel. The deep countersunk crown is far less vulnerable to damage than a flat crown. If you do not like the 60-degree countersunk crown, it is easily possible to turn the outside of the muzzle end of the barrel parallel for 3 inches. The barrel may then be set back into the three-jawed chuck on the lathe and the countersunk area turned off to produce a flat crown. Another way to do this is to grab the shank in the chuck, while supporting the muzzle in a steady rest. If a barrel lacks the ultimate edge in accuracy, the first thing to check (and the easiest thing to fix) is the crown at the muzzle. Again, the flat crown has the greatest potential for accuracy but is also the most easily damaged. The final cut of a flat crown should only remove about .004 inch, and it should be taken very slowly with a very sharp tool.

THREADING THE ACTION AND BARREL

There are some readers who will want to thread barrel blanks and screw them into 10/22 receivers. This section describes the process for those who are so inclined.

There was a time when I thought very little of Ruger's barrel retention system. Then, as I spent more time with it, I came to appreciate the speed and ease with which barrels can be changed. I used one action and one scope to test-fire a number of factory barrels. Even when I did not change the scope's zero, I was surprised by how close the various barrels shot to the same point of impact at 50 yards. The two-screw/angled-key, factory barrel retention system binds the barrel at an angle into the receiver, tightening it in a way that must be understood to be appreciated. A threaded-barrel mount may be superior, but I am currently quite happy with Ruger's existing system.

There are some in the accurizing industry who will not mount a barrel in a 10/22 unless it has been threaded. They feel that the only way a 10/22 will reach its true potential is with a threaded barrel. I am not here to argue with them, but I must point out that it is very difficult to tighten a threaded 10/22 barrel into its receiver in a meaningful way. The 6-ounce aluminum receiver is so soft and fragile that you run the risk of either cracking it or stripping its threads if too much torque is put into the system.

I will give a quick overview of the process, and then I will take the process step by step. First, thread the barrel and receiver, and temporarily fit them together. The barrel is marked for the extractor cut and then removed. The cut is machined, and the unit is reassembled for a trial fit. If all goes well, barrel and receiver are taken apart a second time and degreased. Epoxy is spread on the threads, and the unit is assembled for the third and last time.

THREADING THE RECEIVER

The rear cleanout hole is a very useful aid in threading the receiver, and if this has not yet been done, now is the time. Even though it is

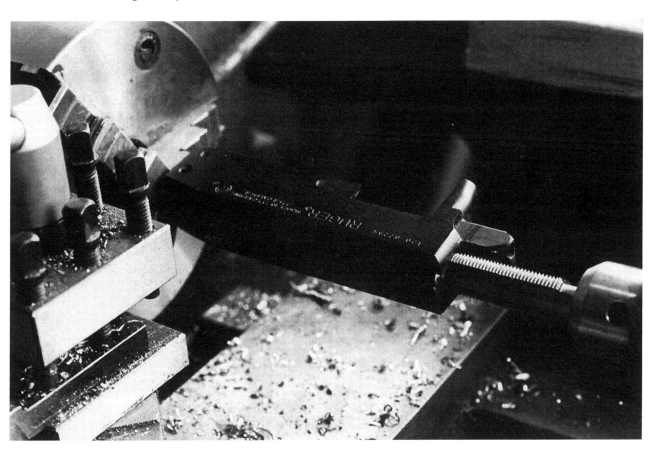

Thread the receiver. Turn the receiver by hand while holding the tap with a chuck in the lathe's tailstock.

possible to jig the receiver for threading in an end mill, more people have lathes available than end mills, so I'll use a lathe and the rear access hole to line up the action for threading.

The hole in the receiver for the 10/22's barrel happens to be about 11/16 inch in diameter, which is the perfect size for a 3/4-20 tap (3/4 inch in diameter, 20 threads per inch). If you don't want to buy a special tap and die for this work, a 3/4-16 NF (national fine) thread is more commonly available. It will work just as well as 3/4-20, providing that the same size thread is also used on the barrel. Most in the industry, however, use the 3/4-20 as the standard for the 10/22. If I were doing only one receiver and barrel I would use 3/4-16. If I expected to do a great number of receivers, I would go to 3/4-20, because that is the current industry standard.

If you have a lathe, threading the receiver is a pretty simple affair. Clamp a pin of the size of the rear access hole in the receiver in the three-jawed chuck of the headstock. Slide the rear of the receiver onto this pin. Clamp the 3/4-inch tap in the tailstock chuck. Lubricate the tap with cutting fluid. Rotate the cast receiver by hand while feeding the tap into the front of the receiver. The aluminum receiver is very soft and threads easily. It should be all over in about two minutes. I was surprised at how easily the first receiver went.

TURNING THE BARREL

Assuming the barrel is a blank, it should first be inspected and then cut to rough length. By now you probably know that I tend to favor short barrels for the .22 LR. I believe they are more accurate because they are inherently stiffer and thus more resistant to vibration. In addition, my testing has told me that I get maximum velocity from a 16-inch barrel. Benchrest competition of the highest order is usually carried out with fairly short barrels. I recommend that the blank be cut to between 17 and 18 inches in length, which will allow a margin for errors and mistakes.

That done, both ends should be faced off square in the lathe. Most blanks have bores that are tighter on one end. The muzzle end should be tighter. By convention, the stamping of bore size and twist rate is usually done on the end of the barrel that is tighter.

The next step is to counterbore the ends for a 60-degree live center. Because most blanks are quite rough on the outside, the process may be done in one of two ways. The first (and some say the best) way is to use a piloted counterbore. Here, the barrel is clamped in a vise, and the bore is deburred with a knife or a deburring tool. At this point I usually run a cleaning patch or two through the bore to remove any grit or abrasive debris that could damage the pilot or the cutting edges of the counterbore. The land diameter (minimum bore diameter) is then measured. A pilot of the appropriate size is then slipped on the end of the counterbore (pilots are available in graduations of .0005 or .0002 inch). I use cutting fluid and a 3/8-inch electric drill motor to place small counterbores in each end of the blank. The depth of each counterbore is about 3/16 inch, which is more than enough for sufficient bearing on the live center in the tailstock. The process may sound complicated, but once one is set up, it should take less than a minute.

As mentioned elsewhere, another method of getting the counterbore is to grip just the tip of one end of the barrel blank in the headstock chuck. A regular center drill can be slowly advanced into the barrel while the headstock is turned by hand. Feed slowly, using a new, sharp bit and plenty of cutting oil. If the barrel was faced off perfectly square, the center drill will center itself perfectly in the bore—but if the bore is not square, serious eccentricity will develop. I have had perfect results using this method, but the ends of the barrel *must* be square. You must use proper feel when advancing the bit in the tailstock. Never use the lathe's motor when doing this operation because the bit will wander and chatter. This method *demands* excellence in its execution.

Many .22 LR blanks will range from 1 to 1 1/4 inch in diameter. For the 10/22, the rear portion will need to be turned down to about .920 inch. First, grab one end of the blank by only 1/4 inch in the tips of the jaws of the chuck. Advance and set the live center of the tailstock in the other end of the barrel. Turn the diameter near the tailstock just enough to clean it up. Reverse the barrel in the lathe and clean up the other end, again working at the tailstock. Do this a third time, and the barrel will probably be rotating true with its bore. Some who turn barrels only turn between two centers, using a dog to drive the barrel. If the stud in the dog is tightened too much it will raise a bump in the bore. Be careful if you use this method. Either method will result in an outer diameter that is fairly concentric with the bore.

Once both ends are true the barrel can be brought down close to its finished size of .920 inch. The barrel will probably turn out to be cylindrical. A variation of that will have a larger diameter near the muzzle. This will probably induce a slight choke at the muzzle, which I am very much in favor of. One could also taper the barrel, but if a tapered barrel is desired, why not use an original Ruger factory barrel?

All this may sound complex and labor intensive, but once you're set up for it, truing the barrel and turning to finish size probably won't take more than 15 minutes. If the barrel is longer and thinner and tapered, very light cuts will be necessary to avoid chatter.

For most of my turning, I use a holder with 3/8-inch, triangular, positive-rake inserts. Since it has three cutting tips, each insert can be rotated three times. I have tried triangular, negative-rake inserts (which have essentially six cutting tips), but they cause excessive pressure when cutting, which is unacceptable for turning a barrel. You want to take barrel material off with a minimum of cutting pressure and deformation.

I buy most of my lathe cutting tools from MSC (see Appendix A for supply sources) and have been able to do most of my barrel work with a single right-handed, 1/2-inch shank tool holder. This bears industry-standard lettering: MTGN. I use 1/8-inch-thick, flat-ground, 3/8-inch TPG (triangle, positive-rake) inserts of C6 carbide. The grades, as far as I can tell, start at C2, which is the softest and toughest. The hardest grade is C6, and I buy mine with a titanium nitride coating, which is gold in color.

For very fine work, or where I might encounter chatter, I will use an insert with a 1/64-inch tip radius. This is a very fine point and is easily broken, so I don't use it often. For most general turning, I use an insert with a 1/32-inch tip radius. This radius contacts more surface area, is more prone to chatter, and holds up much better. The broadest insert has a 3/64-inch tip radius. This is very tough and long lasting, gives a very uniform surface, and is the most prone to chatter. These bits cost from $3 to $6 each, which makes each cutting tip cost from $1 to $2. Occasionally, imported inserts go on sale from MSC for $1 each, and I buy them by the hundreds.

Forty years ago I ground all my own bits. Today, these carbide inserts are real time savers. Because they are very consistent and versatile, they are almost all I currently use. If I am careful, don't take more than .020 inch at a cut, and hit the barrel with a light touch of cutting oil before each pass, I can turn two or three barrels with a single point on an insert. I am told that an air-oil mist system extends tool life even more. If I'm turning stainless steel I can turn one barrel, but it may take two points. Life is short. The carbide inserts are well worth the money.

At one time I gave all barrel surfaces a fine finish and a brilliant polish. Lately, I have gone in the other direction and deliberately leave some roughness and tool marks on the surface of the barrel so it will take blueing, Parkerizing, or a baked-on coating even better. Let your taste be your guide here. Don't do any polishing until the last of the machine work is done.

TURNING THE SHANK

Once the barrel is a parallel cylinder about .920 inch in diameter, I turn a shank on the breech end about 7/8 inch long and a little less than 3/4 inch in diameter. You may leave the

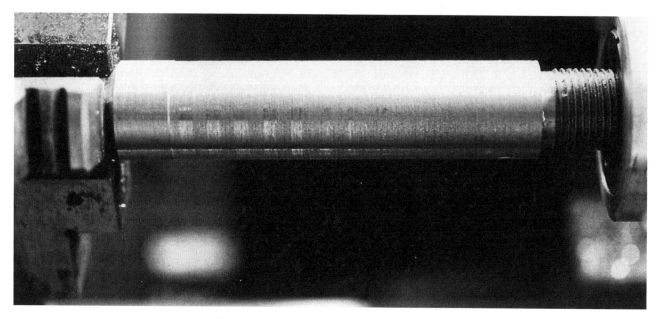

Optional: Turn and thread a new barrel blank.

shank a full 3/4 inch (.750 inch) in diameter, but that would choke the die, resulting in torn threads and difficult turning. Machinists have wrestled with this for years. Testing has revealed that threads that are only about 75-percent deep are fully as strong as 100-percent threads, so that's what the industry has embraced. Correspondingly, the shank should be turned to about .735 inch, which will allow a die to form perfect 75-percent threads with relative ease.

If you are going to use a single-point cutting tool on the lathe to make those threads, now is the time. In either case, it is a good idea to reduce the diameter of the shank to about .715 inch for 1/8 inch near the shoulder. That will allow tool movement at the time of threading and thread clearance when it is time to screw the barrel into the action. If the barrel won't screw all the way in, taking a little more off the shank diameter near the shoulder will help. When cutting threads single-point it is a good plan to turn the lathe slowly, in back gear, and to spin the barrel in reverse. You can then start each cut near the shoulder, with the bit held upside down in the tool holder. This way, there will be no need to

panic when the bit approaches the shoulder (running the bit into the shoulder will break the bit and damage the blank). The cutting tool will be moving the other way, simply going off the shank and into space as the tool finishes each pass.

I have made a fixture to hold the appropriate die in my tool carriage. Before threading, I first machine a 45-degree bevel on the tip of the shank. This helps guide the die over the shank, encouraging it to dig in and start cutting right away. I always use sufficient cutting oil and rotate the headstock by hand to thread the shank. The slowest speed in back gear could be used for some of this threading, with the last 1/4 inch finished by hand. Cutting the screw threads single-point is probably better for concentricity but is more time consuming.

Once the threads are cut, I check the fit by screwing the action on while the barrel is still in the headstock. If all is well, the shank may then be faced off to the appropriate length, which is exactly 3/4 of an inch. If the fit is too tight, another pass can be made with the single-point set a touch deeper. If an adjustable split-die is used, it can be adjusted to cut deeper threads.

CHAMBERING

The barrel may be chambered in the lathe, but I usually use a variable-speed, 3/8-inch electric drill motor because it gives me a better feel. If the chamber reamer runs out of oil or packs up with chips, you can't feel it on the powerful lathe. You have a better chance of feeling it with a hand-held electric drill. Some turn the reamer by hand, but, again, this seems to dull the cutting edges prematurely.

I use a Bentz .22 LR reamer made and sold by Clymer or sold by Brownells. Do not use a match reamer made for a bolt gun, because there isn't enough clearance. Feeding and extraction will be very difficult with a finished chamber reamed to match dimensions. The Bentz reamer is more funnel shaped, being larger in the back to allow easy insertion and extraction and tight at the throat for accuracy. The angle of the leade at the throat is extremely shallow.

Many reamers have a solid pilot, which will work for most barrels. Blanks made by Lothar Walther, however, often have an unusually small minor diameter. A standard pilot will not fit the bore, and you will thus have to purchase a reamer with a smaller removable pilot or have a solid pilot ground down to fit. These barrels are often extremely accurate, and the extremely tight bore may have something to do with that accuracy.

I clamp my turned barrel in a padded vise, chuck the appropriate reamer in my drill motor, and I'm ready to go. I use a good cutting oil and rotate the reamer at a slow speed. I go about a third of the way and then withdraw the rotating reamer. All chips are thoroughly removed from the oily reamer with a soft paper towel, and I run a patch through the bore to clear the swarf from the chamber area. I then oil both chamber and reamer and go in again, taking great care to let the pilot lead the way. It would not do to introduce axial misalignment. The second pass

Chamber the barrel with a Bentz reamer.

gets me two-thirds of the way in. I again clean the reamer carefully and run another patch down and out the bore.

At this point I put a live round into the chamber of the barrel, using the same brand or type as that which would probably be used by the owner (a dummy round would not do: there is considerable variation between types and brands of ammunition). Then I carefully note just how much farther I will need to go. I remove the round and mark the reamer with a Sharpie marking pen. I am very careful at this stage and go just a little farther. The bore is again cleaned, and I try the live round again until I feel a very small amount of resistance just before the round chambers fully. I stop at this point. Firelapping and natural wear will deepen the chamber a little more.

Some will not be comfortable in driving a reamer with an electric drill. They are welcome to use a lathe but are advised to use a floating chamber reamer holder. This has some slop built into the rear end that allows the reamer to stay lined up with a bore that is unlikely to run true as it turns. An exaggerated analogy is to try to ream a hole in the handle of a jump rope while someone is using it.

As you get close to the proper depth, you may want to abandon the drill and do the rest of the chamber by hand, because it is very easy to go too far too fast. The work will go much slower, allowing much better control.

Barrelmaker LaBounty tells of inserting a tight, perfectly parallel pin in a rifled bore. Using a dial indicator, it is virtually impossible to get the pin to turn perfectly true as the barrel is rotated in the headstock. A hand-held reamer or a floating reamer holder are the only ways to get a chamber that is properly lined up with the bore.

THE EXTRACTOR SLOT

Clamp the receiver between wooden blocks in a heavy vise. Screw the barrel tightly into the receiver. Be careful when doing this. The receiver is not very strong: it is easily cracked, and the aluminum threads are easily stripped. A strap wrench should be used to grab the barrel without damaging it. Unscrew the barrel a turn and then tighten it again. Do this a few times. Unlike a steel receiver, the 10/22's aluminum receiver has little or no spring to it, so the threads must be worn in a little. If this is not done properly, the threads will give a little on the final installation, causing the extractor cut to be in the wrong place.

Take a sharp scribe and make a witness mark on both the barrel and receiver after they are tightened. You want to be able to return to that exact same position later. Take a marking pen or a bit of Prussian blue, and put a touch of color on the rear face of the barrel, where the extractor should fall. Clamp the receiver upside down so that you can access the inside. Insert the bolt (without the operating handle and spring) and move it back and forth inside the receiver so that it lightly strikes the rear of the barrel. Eventually, a small mark will form where the extractor rubs the barrel. Use the scribe to clearly mark this spot. Remove the barrel.

If you have an end mill, a 1/8-inch key slot cutter may be used to make the extractor cut. If not, a file will serve. File close to the rear of the chamber but do not cut into it. After filing, I would use a small grindstone in a Dremel tool to put a little hollow into the extractor slot. That hollow will allow the extractor to make better contact with the rim of each shell. If the key slot cutter was used, the hollow will already be there.

Screw the barrel back in and check the fit. A wise person would assemble the action and fire several rounds to make sure that everything functions as it should. Take the barrel out again.

HARDENING THE REAR OF THE BARREL

Hardening can be done with the very hot flame of an acetylene torch. Turn down a little stub on the piece of barrel blank you cut off. This will be used to practice on. A 3/4-inch-diameter stub about 3/8-inch long will serve. Use a fairly large torch and get the flame quite hot. You want a lot of heat in a very short period because you only want to harden about .03-inch of the rear face. Hold the practice piece in a pair of pliers. Play the flame against the rear of the stub for about 5 seconds. Do this in dim light, not in full sunlight. As soon as a red color begins to appear on the rear face, immediately quench the barrel stub in either oil or water. Try oil first. Shut the torch off and try a file on the barrel stub. Only the rear face should be hard. If the surface isn't hard enough, repeat the heating sequence and quench in cold water. Saltwater removes heat even more rapidly; hence, it is more effective.

If all went well, repeat the exercise with your 10/22's barrel. A blacksmith or an experienced knifemaker should be able to do this job in less than a minute. Again, only the rear face should be hard. The second and third turn of threads should be soft. If the rear face turns out so hard that it could shatter, put the entire barrel in a kitchen oven. Bring the heat up to about 400°F. Shut the oven down and allow the barrel to cool slowly, over a period of an hour or two. This will draw the hardness a bit, allowing the rear of the barrel to be hard but tough.

CROWNING THE BARREL

As mentioned earlier, I have successfully used a properly executed countersink as the final crown. I have not found a 60-degree countersink to be less accurate than any other type of crown. Inspect the area under a strong hand lens to ensure that it is symmetrical. I often use a bamboo skewer to feel all around the bore/crown transition to ensure that there are no burrs.

(A very long article on barrel crowns appeared in a 1996 issue of *Precision Shooting* magazine.) They did quite a number of things to a barrel's muzzle, but in the end they finally ran a 60-degree countersink into the muzzle to finish the job. Such a crown is well protected. It is least likely to be damaged by a careless person with a cleaning rod or by resting the muzzle against the ground or pavement.

Flat crowns and 11-degree crowns are also popular. As discussed earlier, a flat crown can be made by putting the barrel into a three-jawed chuck in a lathe. Using a new, sharp bit, make a cut across the face of the muzzle to clean it up. Make a 45-degree bevel on the outer edge of the muzzle to soften the transition between the face of the muzzle and the cylinder of the barrel. This will ease the process of inserting the completed firearm into a gun case. It could also prevent a nasty cut if you ever accidentally bump into the barrel. Take a scrap of fine, 400-grit sandpaper and gently touch the muzzle of the spinning barrel to smooth things up. Do all necessary lathe work on the barrel before permanently inserting it into the action. Most lathes will not accommodate the barrel afterward.

POLISHING THE BARREL

If you want a polished surface, the barrel is now ready for this phase. Put the barrel back in the lathe, holding it in the three-jawed chuck by the last 2 or 3 inches. Cover the bed of the lathe with a piece of cardboard to keep grit off the ways. Start with 100-grit and then move on to about 220, which will get things about as smooth as you could want. I use a sheet of sandpaper about 6 inches square. If things get too hot to hold, a few sheets of paper toweling will provide some insulation. With most of the barrel smooth, turn it around and work on the other end. Use a piece of heavy paper to protect the polished surface from the jaws of the chuck. I use those little insert sections found in most magazines because they are thick, tough, and contain little or no filler. Take care to blend the transition where the barrel wasn't sanded before. A stainless barrel may be left polished. Some people use polishing compound on stainless barrels, but a mirror finish is the last thing I would want on a firearm.

The barrel can just as easily be bead blasted, which will provide a smooth matte surface. Sand blasting will yield a rougher surface. Either of these will provide a good base for blueing, or

Parkerizing, or three coats of black, brown, or green baking lacquers. If you opt for the lacquer, wait until the barrel is in the receiver so that you can spray them both at the same time. Put a little wood or rubber plug in the muzzle to protect the crown/bore transition from bead blast material or paint buildup.

GLUING THE THREADED BARREL IN

Degrease the threads on the barrel and receiver with carburetor cleaner. Put a dab of wheel bearing grease into the rear of the chamber to prevent epoxy from adhering to the chamber walls. Mix a very small amount of Brownells Acraglass, J.B. Weld, or Two-Ton epoxy. Mix thoroughly and apply to both the barrel's and receiver's threads. Screw the barrel into the receiver. Make sure that the witness marks line up. Oil the face of the bolt and put it into the action. Make sure the extractor falls into its slot in the barrel. Clean off excess epoxy with a paper towel and a little acetone. Let it sit for 24 hours at 70°F to achieve a full cure. Don't forget to run a patch down the bore before firing the weapon.

A LIGHTER, MORE COMPACT 10/22

Some people don't need a 10/22 for extreme accuracy; they simply want a rifle for survival or protection. Sometimes the extra weight and bulk of the factory rifle are disadvantages. Although some people might carry a .22 pistol for its compactness and portability, few pistols are as inherently accurate as a rifle, even a compact rifle. A rifle with a plastic folding stock and a shorter barrel would be a major improvement in portability.

There is a legal problem with attaching a folding stock to a 10/22 rifle that was manufactured after the enactment of the Brady Bill in the summer of 1994.

It is my understanding that our government can't legislate against existing firearms; therefore, you must only fit folding stocks to 10/22 receivers manufactured before the summer of 1994. Both Choate and Butler Creek make (or have made) folding stocks that are sturdy and of good quality. I would trust either of these stocks on a .22 LR survival rifle on which my life depended.

There is also a legal concern with regard to rifles with barrels shorter than 16 inches. A 1934 federal law levied a tax of $200 each on the civilian ownership of machine guns, silencers, and short-barreled rifles. The tax on short-barreled shotguns (under 18 inches and without a buttstock) is only $5. Because of the Second Amendment to the U.S. Constitution, it was not possible in 1934 to prohibit the ownership of these devices, so the lawyers and legislators worked out a restriction (taxation) they could enforce. Sixty years later we're still laboring under this 1934 restriction. Before talking about shortening rifle barrels below 16 inches, it is my duty to inform you that a $200 tax is due, and that certain additional federal and state restrictions may also apply.

Usually a 16 1/2-inch barrel will prove to be an ideal length for a .22. However, there are times when one wants a rifle to be as short and small as possible. In terms of accuracy and striking power, there is no practical difference between a 12-inch and a 24-inch barrel. A 10-inch barrel on a 10/22 with a folding stock will make a survival package about 18 inches long. You shouldn't go much shorter than 10 inches because of the danger of shooting yourself in the finger of the weak hand during a moment of inattention.

I have occasionally made up registered short-barreled 10/22s for bush pilots needing survival rifles for their bailout packs, which they are required by law to carry when flying in remote areas of Alaska. A plain, short, stainless-steel barrel about 10 inches long is very handy. If the arm is suppressed, a 6-inch ported barrel inside a 12-inch-long tube is about right. The table in the chapter on barrels gives the velocities you can expect with a given barrel length and various types of ammunition. If you want more velocity, an 8-inch barrel inside a slightly larger suppressor will provide it.

THE LIGHTWEIGHT BARREL

The practice of drawing 4130, seamless, chrome-moly steel over a mandrel is an art that has been carefully developed over the years. It is possible to order 4130 steel tubing in almost any inside and outside diameter at a very reasonable price. A few have taken to developing special (slightly larger diameter) carbide rifling buttons that may be drawn through short sections of this steel tubing to rifle it. These sections of tubing are then used as inexpensive barrel liners, some of which can be fairly accurate. One liner has an OD of .312 (5/16) inch. This is a bit thin for dependability. Ranch Products has been experimenting with a barrel using a liner of well over .4 inch, which is very sturdy.

The barrel liner serves as the core of the aftermarket, lightweight composite barrel. A liner is either soldered or epoxied into a short steel or aluminum barrel stub. The remainder is covered with aluminum, thermoplastic, composite fiberglass, or composite carbon fiber, resulting in barrels that are remarkably light. While a few of these barrels exhibit fair accuracy, I doubt that they'll ever be adopted by the benchrest crowd. A very small percentage of the composite barrels will deliver a cold, 3-shot group under 1/2 inch at 50 yards. The remainder can be expected to group from 2 to 6 inches at that same distance.

Most of the lightweight barrels cost less than $50. Those turned from a single steel blank and sheathed in carbon fiber approach $500. As any of these barrels heat up they are prone to walking their shots around the target face. Although ultimate accuracy is often lacking, the lightweight feature will sometimes outweigh other disadvantages.

The tensioned barrels are also lightweight, but they tend to be much stiffer and far more accurate. They are almost always made from a heavy blank and can use stee, carbon fiber, or aluminum for the compression tube.

IMPULSE COMPENSATORS

Why, one might ask, would one want a compensator on a .22? Most stocks are configured with the axis of the bore placed about 4 inches above the center of the buttplate on the stock. For a right-handed person, when a rifle is discharged the departing bullet and gas cause an equal and opposite reaction against the barrel and action. This in turn acts against the stock, which pivots around your shoulder and body mass. The bottom line is that the barrel tends to move up and somewhat to the right for a right-handed shooter. When the trigger is pulled the muzzle rises and turns, taking the scope off the target and preventing you from actually seeing the bullet strike. A proper muzzle compensator captures some of the escaping gas in a reservoir, redirecting it to counter muzzle movement. Regulating the direction and amount of gas released is an art, since barrel and stock configurations will vary.

The act of firing a properly compensated rifle is a luxury for some, but a very real asset. For someone such as a police sniper, it should be a necessity. A police sniper may only take one or two important shots during his lifetime. It is absolutely critical that he see that shot strike through the scope, so he can determine whether follow-up action will need to be taken and be able to report the correct facts to his supervisor. Normally, some recoil will remain on the 10/22, but muzzle rise and twist will disappear, and the scope will stay on target. For a hunter or someone who shoots at action targets such as falling plates or mini-pins, a compensator is a valuable asset.

The idea of a compensator has been around for at least 70 years, but only recently have all the forces been properly understood. A past article in *Machine Gun News* touted a compensator of my design, and that prompted a number of requests from owners of 10/22 machine guns. It took a number of trips to a local range to get a design properly regulated, but I now have a system that will allow a shooter to stay on target during a 30- to 50-round burst.

There are several properties of a successful compensator that bear mentioning. The most important is a reservoir that holds and traps a quantity of propellant gas. This allows a more constant flow, which in turn generates a longer push, rather than a quick jab without follow-through. The hole in the muzzle end of the compensator should be perfectly concentric and just large enough to allow free and easy passage for a bullet. Often designers try to make a compensator of the same size and contour as the barrel. This is a mistake, since the slender contour usually lacks the necessary volume. It also requires the muzzle of the barrel to be turned to a smaller diameter to make room for a shoulder and threads. The smaller diameter often causes the bore to expand at the muzzle—which, as we now know, is detrimental to accuracy. If a shoulder is turned, the fit of the compensator is often less than perfect at this shoulder, causing a slight kink in the bore as the compensator is torqued on. Last, but not least, most designers try to make their compensators suitable for both the left- and right-handed shooter. Unfortunately, you can't have it both ways. Some designers make a series of holes radially, and this blows gas in all directions. If the arm is shot from the prone position, the gas will blow dirt, dust, and stones in all directions. Other designers drill their holes in the vertical direction. This will keep the muzzle down, but the barrel will still swing left or right.

For a right-handed shooter, most of the gas should flow in a 2 o'clock direction. For a left-handed shooter, gas should flow in a 10 o'clock direction. The caliber, volume of gas, and weight of the firearm all have bearing on the size of the reservoir required and the size and direction of the gas port. Most manufacturers drill multiple gas ports, while others drill only one. Others electrodischarge machine (EDM) their gas ports in some unusual shape. The shape and number of holes in a compensator mean nothing—it is volume and direction that are important. An EDM hole can cause problems, since the spark erosion process microheats and hardens the edges of the hole. I have seen more than one large-caliber compensator break and fly apart because

of a crack that started at one of these EDM holes. A drilled or abraded hole doesn't look as fancy, but it's more likely to hold together.

It should be mentioned again that the hole in the end of the compensator should be perfectly concentric with the bore. A bullet will "feel" advancing gas pressure caused by an eccentric hole and respond with a lack of stability and accuracy.

In terms of attachment, I make every effort to avoid threading the end of a barrel. Plain steel may be soft-soldered. I turn only a few thousandths off the exterior to obtain concentricity and then bore the compensator about .001-inch *larger* to leave room for the solder. With enough surface area, a good flux, and proper soldering technique, this can be a very secure attachment.

With the passage of the Brady Act in 1994, threading the muzzle of a rifle barrel can be a problem. This technique avoids that problem. A hard, low-temperature silver solder is available for large-bore weapons and the greater forces involved. When using stainless I usually machine the muzzle to be about .0025 inch *larger* than the inside diameter of the compensator. I then use a touch of red Loctite and drive the compensator on with a mallet. If the fit is too tight, the compensator will have to be heated to about 900°F before being quickly driven on. For a .22 this press fit will provide a bit of choke to the muzzle, which I feel will be an advantage.

If threads are used, they should be cut with a single point on the lathe and should not take very much diameter from the outside of the muzzle. Loctite will hold the compensator in place if threads are used. For a barrel with right-handed twist rifling, left-handed threads should be used. With right-handed threads, the barrel will try to unscrew itself from the compensator with each shot. This is a major problem with large-caliber rifles.

Although it is much harder to do so, I usually place the hole(s) in the side of the compensator *after* it has been attached to the barrel. I usually test-fire first to ensure that the crown and bore are accurate. An end mill works well for boring the hole. If, after testing, you determine that the hole needs to be moved a bit, the end mill can be used to enlarge that hole to one side. A full-auto burst out of a machine gun will really let you know how effectively a compensator is performing.

It should be mentioned that some try to reduce recoil by slanting or angling the gas escape holes to the rear. In most cases this is a waste of effort. For the .50 BMG, a clamshell recoil reducer appears to be moderately effective at this task. Smaller calibers don't normally require such an active approach to redirecting gases.

The sound pressure wave delivered to the shooter's face and ear will be greatly increased by any compensator. Extensive testing in Finland and the United States has indicated an increase of roughly 8 decibels. That may not seem like much, but it represents a sound pressure magnitude more than 60 times greater. Ear protection is mandatory.

DISASSEMBLY, CLEANING, AND REASSEMBLY

4

I should state at the outset that I take a firearm apart as little as possible. I don't clean a weapon each time it is used because that wears out screws and fittings before their time. Having said that, there are times when you must take something apart to clean it properly and to lubricate the moving parts.

INITIAL TESTING OF THE RIFLE

Obstruction Test

Before I do anything with a brand-new firearm I first run a wooden dowel down its bore to make sure that there are no obstructions. With the 10/22, I hold the opened action and its ejection port to a light source and then peer down the bore. If I can't see the light, I'll take a wooden dowel 1/8- or 3/16-inch in diameter and drop it down the bore. I may also ram a #1 cotton patch through to prove to my satisfaction that no lumps of grease are waiting to bulge the

barrel when the first bullet surges through. That done, I'll take the rifle to a firing range to do a function test.

Function Test

Once at the range, or in front of the bullet trap in my shop, I will run a full magazine of ammunition through the rifle. I first load five rounds of slow, target-velocity ammunition into the magazine, followed by five rounds of generic, high-speed ammo from Wal-Mart or K-Mart. When I actually fire the gun the high-speed ammo comes out first because it was loaded last. If the 10/22 in question is a brand-new firearm it may be stiff at first, and the high-speed ammo will have the extra power to function the bolt smartly. Most of the 10/22s I have tested operate properly, but many fail to feed or fail to eject the milder .22 LR loads. If the firearm fails to fire or won't shoot accurately, I send it back to the manufacturer. There is little to be gained by trying to repair a major flaw, which is clearly the responsibility of the manufacturer.

Safety Test

I also give the firearm a little safety test before I start to work on it. First, I point it downrange and try to pull the trigger with the safety on. After having tried that, while the arm is still pointing in a safe direction, I take the safety off. If the hammer drops with the safety on, or by itself after the safety is released, the firearm fails the test. I also do a butt-slam simulation to see whether the hammer will drop if the gun is dropped. *After making sure that the gun is unloaded*, I guide the rifle so that it drops on its buttplate to a rubber mat on the floor from about 2 feet. I am careful not to hurt the firearm and hold it during its descent so that it doesn't fall sideways. If any firearm fails the safety test, I send it back to the factory for repair, with a detailed note explaining the problem.

FACTORY RETURNS

If a firearm has a serious flaw it is always best to find out early in the game, so it can be sent to the manufacturer for correction before the owner starts to invest time and emotion. I once bought a new Ruger 77/22 rifle that absolutely would not fire. I also once bought a new MK II stainless pistol that delivered 8-foot groups at 25 yards. Both firearms were returned to the factory. Ruger replaced them with fully functional firearms and an apology.

If you are tempted to return a modified firearm to the factory, be advised that any nonstandard parts will be removed and destroyed. If you had a spring kit or an expensive Volquartsen titanium hammer and firing pin installed, they will be removed and trashed—to be replaced with standard Ruger parts. Do not send a barreled action in with an aftermarket stock. If you had a trigger that pulled a crisp 40 ounces in your 10/22 and returned it to the factory repair shop, it would come back with a gritty, hammer-cocking 14 pounds when returned. I am not

saying this with bitterness. I just want you to know what to expect beforehand.

It is against federal law to ship a loaded firearm in the mail. Make absolutely certain that the chamber and magazine are empty before mailing a firearm. Federal law permits you, as a private citizen, to return your personal firearm to the factory for repair or refinishing, but state laws vary. Some permit it, and some don't. Federal law also permits you to receive that same firearm when it is returned to you. You can mail a barreled action to the Ruger factory (Sturm, Ruger & Co., Service Department, 411 Sunapee St., Newport, NH 03773). Always include a letter with your name, address, phone number, and instructions detailing what you want done to the 10/22 rifle. Insure the package for full value.

Federal law does not permit shipping a pistol through the U.S. Postal System unless the shipper and the receiver both hold Federal Firearms Licenses. If the post office X-rays the package and discovers that an unlicensed individual has sent a pistol, the pistol will be confiscated and that individual will be in trouble. If you want to return a pistol, use United Parcel Service or Federal Express. Wrap the weapon in cardboard and secure with strapping tape. Insure for full value and hold on to the receipt. With the present state of our country, it is entirely possible than any firearm, shipped by any means, will get stolen en route. Pistols should be sent to the following address: Sturm, Ruger & Co., Service Department, Ruger Road, Prescott, AZ 86301-6105.

REFINISHING

Ruger will refinish the metal work of a rifle or a pistol for a modest fee. Remember that the receiver, trigger group, and barrel band on the 10/22 are all painted aluminum. Only its barrel is of blued steel. If the barrel has had over 90,000 rounds through it you might be better off replacing the barrel ($40, plus shipping) rather than bothering to refinish it.

Many people have had their 10/22s for a long time or inherited them from a loved one and have developed an affection for their particular weapons. Rather than buy a new firearm, they want to clean the old one up and continue to use it. I can certainly respect that. Others have no special affection for a particular weapon; they are just trying to save a little money. A friend who is a gun dealer tells me that some people will drive a thousand miles in order to save $5. Only you know which class you fall into.

In areas where the atmosphere is damp, salty, or corrosive, you might be better off with a Parkerized barrel finish (which is tough and holds oil very well) or with one of the baked-on black finishes currently available through area gunsmiths. I refinished one of my favorite .22 LR bolt guns with baked-on black lacquer from Brownells. I can now pick it up by its barrel without fear of corrosion on a damp day. There are many new finishes developed each year. Some of them are very attractive and durable. A light sandblast (or more gentle bead blast) will prepare the metal for proper paint adhesion. The days of highly polished, reflective finishes have passed.

Ruger does not normally refinish gun stocks (to my knowledge). It is less expensive to refinish your own stock or to buy a new aftermarket stock. Fortunately, this is a job that is easily within the capabilities of most gun owners. Refer to the section on stocks for a thorough treatment of the subject.

DISASSEMBLY

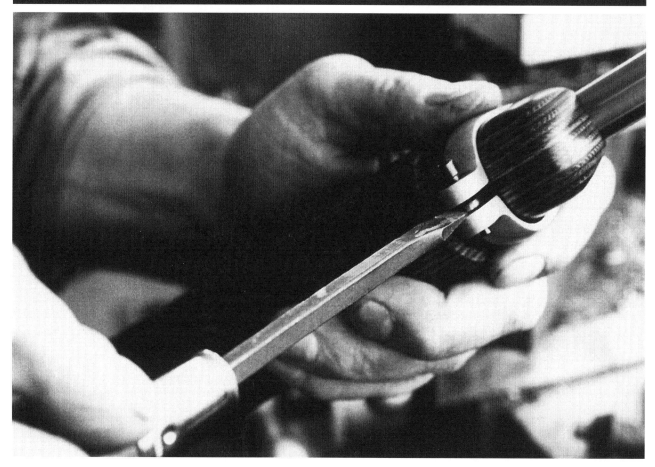

Remove the barrel band by loosening the screw and prying the band apart by twisting with blade of a medium-sized screwdriver.

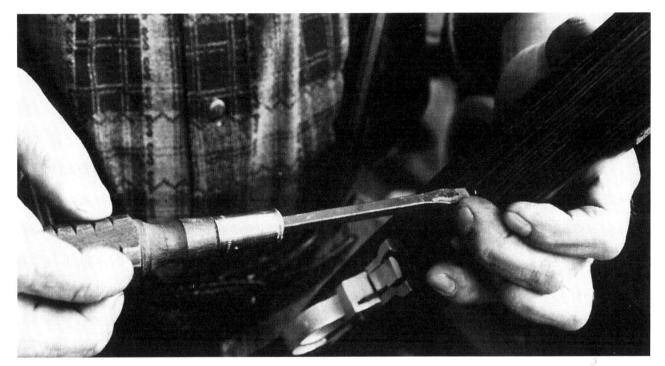

Remove the single action screw.

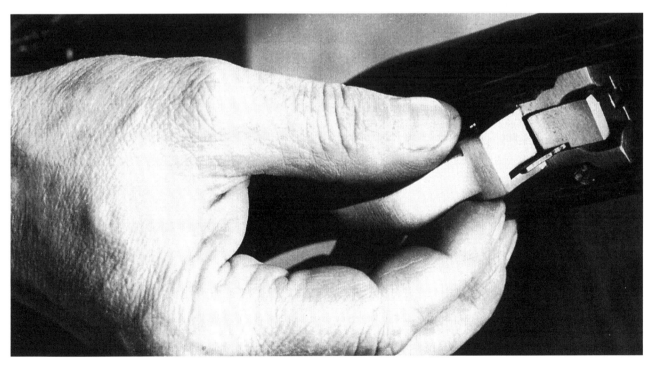

Move the safety to the center position while lifting the front of the barrel/receiver from the stock.

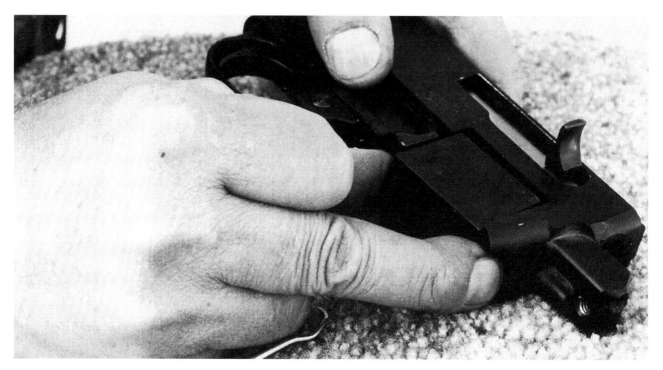

Remove the magazine from the receiver. The barrel was removed in this photo to do other work.
We don't recommend removing the barrel unless it is absolutely necessary.

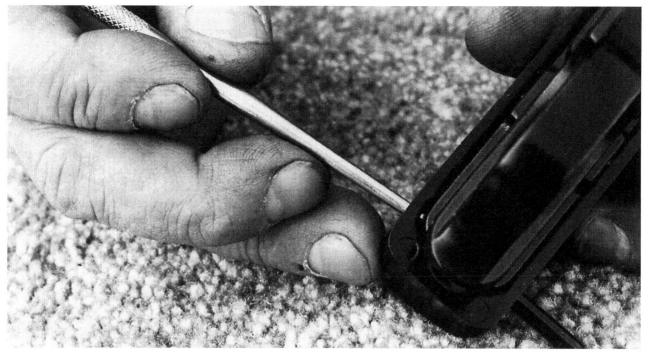

Remove the three largest pins from the receiver. Do not remove any other pins at this time.
The pins will need to be tapped out of a new rifle. They will literally fall out of a used rifle.

Remove the bolt by forcing it to the rear and prying the front up with a screwdriver.
The bolt will not come out unless the 1/4-inch-diameter bolt stop pin has been removed first!

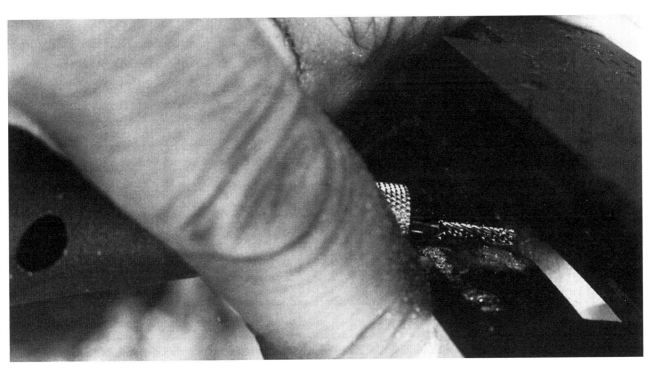

On some receiver castings the lip holding the bolt in place is too long, making bolt removal difficult or impossible.
This photo shows a Dremel tool being used to remove some of the lip from the receiver casting.

Remove the pin holding the hammer in the trigger group.

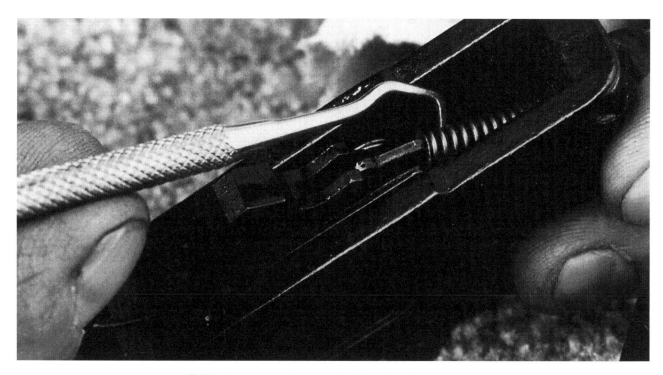

Pull the hammer spring and strut from the trigger group.

Pull the hammer out of the trigger group. Remove spring and inserts from the hammer assembly.

First, always check to ensure that the firearm is unloaded and that the bolt is locked open. The basic model of the 10/22 comes with a barrel band, and this must be removed first. Remove the screw, which pinches the bottom of the band together. Insert a small- to medium-sized screwdriver into the seam between the two bottom halves and gently twist. This will enlarge the band, allowing it to slip forward off the stock without scratching the finish. Be careful: the band is cast aluminum, and some of them snap in two quite easily.

The next step is to back out, or remove, the single screw holding the barreled action into the stock with a medium-sized screwdriver. This done, hold the stock butt down, and gently separate the barrel from the fore-end. While doing this with one hand, manipulate the cross-bolt safety with the other so that equal amounts of the bolt project from the trigger group. The safety is the major impediment to removing the action from the stock. Sometimes it takes some

serious manipulation to get the action out without damaging the stock.

Once the action is out, lay the stock aside. Set the barreled action on a scrap of carpet or an opened newspaper on a table in good light. Remove the 10/22's magazine. There are two 3/16-inch pins that hold the trigger group into the action. On a new gun these will have to be poked out with a nail or a small screwdriver. On a used gun they will fall on the floor (a real problem) as soon as the receiver is removed from the stock. Once the two pins are removed, the trigger group will literally fall from the receiver. Lay the trigger group aside. We will deal with it later.

The last thing to come out of the receiver will be the bolt. Almost everything in the action pivots on or is held in place with a pin. These pins are primarily held in place by the walls of the stock around the action. Once the stock is removed, these pins will either fall out of their own accord or can be poked out with a small punch and a mallet. The last major retaining pin lies in the upper rear of the receiver. It is 1/4 inch in diameter and serves to stop the bolt in its rearward travel. Appropriately, it is called the bolt-stop pin, and it is more sophisticated than would first appear. It rotates slightly and displaces the rear of the bolt slightly when struck in recoil. It looks simple, but it's not. Those pins in a new gun will have to be driven out. In a used 10/22 this pin usually falls out of its own volition. With that pin out, the bolt can usually be drawn to the rear and pivoted out of the receiver. During this process, the bolt handle, recoil spring, and guide rod will usually come loose from the bolt. The guide rod assembly can be removed as a unit by pulling it out of the ejection port. Don't try to take it apart. It is meant to stay together.

Some receivers are cast with their tolerances on the tight side, and it will be difficult to get the bolt out of one of these. If it went in, it should come out, but some bolts are really tough to remove. Again, the bolt *will not* come out if the bolt stop pin remains in the receiver!

There is a small metal rim, which runs parallel to the bottom of the ejection port, and sometimes this goes too far forward to allow easy removal or installation of the bolt. At one time I used to file a little of the forward portion of that rim off to ease the removal process. Now I use a small Dremel tool with a carbide burr to accomplish that same task. If the bolt is tough to remove, that rim or ridge is usually too long. The bolt should drop in and out easily because holding the guide rod/operating handle in place (during reassembly and under spring tension) is hard enough as it is. The aluminum receiver is very soft, so shortening the retention ridge or rim is an easy task. It is hard to believe that this simple operation makes removing and installing the bolt so easy.

CLEANING THE RECEIVER

Once the receiver is empty, it's time to clean things up a bit. If there is a scope, and if it *can* be removed easily, I would take it off so that it doesn't get damaged with cleaning solvent. Some

immerse the receiver and barrel in a parts-cleaning tank, allowing the solvent to remove most of the accumulated powder and bullet lube fouling. I don't have a tank (yet), so I use a spray can of carburetor cleaner, which costs about a dollar at auto parts and other supply houses.

Simply hold the receiver by the barrel and direct a flow into the recess using the long, thin tube that comes with the can. During firing, the act of extracting a spent cartridge from the barrel moves the bolt backward, which sets up a mild positive pressure in the rear of the receiver. This causes most of the crud to build up in the forward part of the bolt. When the bolt flies forward, the action in the rear chamber causes a suction, which pulls some of the slower-moving particles of fouling into the top of the trigger group. Use the carburetor spray outdoors because it is not good to breathe the fumes.

While the inside of the receiver is still wet with solvent, mop as much of the fouling out as you can with a paper towel. This done, it is time for a little detail work. Carburetor cleaner removes most of the oil present in the receiver, so the fouling will be fairly dry. Get a good look at the inside and use a small screwdriver or a dental pick (my favorite tool) to remove all of the accumulated fouling. The area around the barrel will be especially thick, and this is where a small screwdriver, a wire probe, or a dental pick will be especially useful. Once the thick fouling is out, give the inside of the receiver another blast of cleaner and wipe out the last of the material.

CLEANING THE BORE

Some people are passionate (compulsive?) barrel cleaners, often running a patch through their bores after every single shot. If you attempt this with a 10/22 you'll never have any fun. I have shot as many as 10,000 rounds through various .22 LR rifles without ever cleaning their bores.

Very long (24 inches and up) barrels tend to accumulate lead in the last 6 inches or so because the bullets often run dry of lubricant after about

16 inches. Since all of my barrels (and bores) are short and smooth, they do not accumulate lead. In shooting rifles off a bench I find that a barrel often shoots wild after it has been cleaned. It may take from 20 to 150 rounds to fill recesses in the bore that have been scrubbed out by brushes, solvent, patches, and vigorous cleaning.

My experience is not an aberration. All of the BR 50 (.22 LR benchrest at 50 yards) shooters I know experience difficulty after they scrub their bores. One of the problems with the 10/22 is that there is no easy way of cleaning the bore from the rear without taking the barrel out. Removing and replacing the barrel is easy to do, but this single act will probably change the zero on the rifle, and so you will have to adjust your sights again.

I drill a hole in the rear of every 10/22 action I work on (unless a customer specifically requests that I don't). (How to do this is covered in detail in the chapter on actions.) The hole in the rear of the action allows one to roughly adjust the sights by bore-sighting. It also facilitates running the occasional patch through and inspection of the bore.

I regard it as a mortal sin to clean any barrel from its muzzle. The muzzle area is a very fragile thing, easily damaged with a cleaning rod introduced through the muzzle. If you want to clean from the breech, but do not have the rear access hole in the receiver, it is possible to use a stiff nylon strap about 30 inches long and of less than bore diameter. This can be threaded through the chamber via the ejection port and pushed out through the muzzle. A patch or swab is attached to the rear of this strap, and it is pulled through the bore from the muzzle. AMT sells such a strap to be used with its 10/22 clone.

Assuming the rifle has a receiver access hole, it is possible to place a patch that has been dampened with solvent on the rear face of the barrel. I use #1 round flannel cleaning patches from Brownells, which turn out to be about 7/8 inch in diameter. One patch will dampen the chamber area (which is usually the only area that really needs cleaning) and most of the

bore. I use a cleaning rod with the appropriately sized cleaning jag, driven from the rear, down the bore, and out the muzzle. I remove the patch, withdraw the rod, and follow this with about three more dry patches. I always move from breech to muzzle. I never move back and forth in the bore. I only push the patch in the direction the bullets go. I rarely need more than four patches at a go because I don't expect them to come out perfectly clean. I never use stainless or bronze brushes, since these could cause bore damage.

There will be many times when only the chamber area needs cleaning. A bent nylon bore brush can be used through the ejection port to accomplish this task. If the bolt is locked back, no disassembly is necessary. Again, the .22 LR round is self-lubricated, and if proper ammunition is used, little or no cleaning of the rifled bore will be necessary. Each bullet pushes through with its own scouring action. Unfortunately, the cartridge lacks that same scouring action; hence, the chamber will suffer from a buildup of crud, and that buildup will have to be removed from time to time.

CLEANING THE BOLT

Grab the bolt with a pair of pliers and spray it down with a 6-second blast of carburetor cleaner. This done, wipe it down with a paper towel. Don't hold the bolt in your hand while spraying: the cleaner will take natural oils from your skin— which can lead to cracking and peeling skin if done to excess.

Once the bolt is dry, take a small screwdriver or dental pick and go over all surfaces, picking caked accumulations out. The area at the front of the bolt will be especially dirty. A clump usually forms on top of the firing pin slot, and in the recess for the head of the cartridge. The case head area should be cleaned well because an accumulation here will prevent the cartridge from seating fully into the bolt face. This will cause misfires: the firing pin (which is purposely limited in the length of its stroke) won't be able to reach the priming ring when it is struck. Take a small pick and carefully clean the area protected by the extractor. A lot of material accumulates here, and the single extractor prevents it from being seen. The recess in the bolt face averages about .050 inch, and the thickness of the average cartridge rim runs about .042 inch. Some people think the headspace is excessive, but I think it's about right, given the way fouling collects in the corners of the recess.

Once the bolt is picked clean, hit it with another short burst of carburetor cleaner and wipe it down. An old, discarded toothbrush may be useful in scrubbing the underside of the bolt, another area that gets filthy. Don't oil anything yet; we have some inspecting to do.

BOLT HANDLE, GUIDE ROD, AND RECOIL SPRING ASSEMBLY

Take this piece and lightly spray it down, wiping it off quickly with a paper towel. These are small and appear fragile, but I rarely see one damaged. If the spring appears worn or weak, or if the rod is bent, order a new one from Ruger. The entire unit is only $5. Individual pieces are not available. Aftermarket units are available at much higher prices and may or may not be an improvement over the original.

TRIGGER GROUP

The trigger group is fairly simple when taken piece by piece. It is intelligently designed and a marvel of Yankee ingenuity in a compact package. Taken as a whole, it can be confusing to totally understand, especially if you have never seen one in the flesh before. I don't disassemble the trigger group at all when cleaning. (This will be covered in depth in Chapter 5.)

Spray the inside of the group with carburetor cleaner and shake to get some of the particulates out. Here is where a soak in a swirling bath of cleaning solvent will do the most good. Dry the group off with a paper towel and give the insides

a thorough blast with compressed air if you have it. Lay everything aside to dry for an hour or so.

LEAD POISONING

Be sure to thoroughly wash your hands with soap and warm water after the cleaning process. The bolt and receiver area are loaded with very fine lead particles, which can get into your lungs and stomach if you eat without washing your hands. Lead poisoning can be dangerous and debilitating. Take care to keep lead out of your system.

Some people who are extremely sensitive to lead use a dust mask and rubber gloves when they clean firearms. Young people who shoot at indoor ranges should be extremely careful and should at least wear a dust mask while shooting. Lead is present in the vapor form after each discharge. It is also present in most priming mixtures and in particle form as it shears off from pressure on the driving sides of the rifling lands. Young children are extremely susceptible to airborne lead. An integral or muzzle can sound suppressor will capture about 90 percent of this airborne lead, but the remaining 10 percent will still be present. I have seen indoor ranges so thick with haze that shooters had difficulty breathing and seeing the targets. Young people should always be encouraged to wash their hands before eating or drinking after a bout on an indoor firing range.

RE-OILING

If you are not going to work over the trigger group or action at this time but are going to reassemble the 10/22, now is the time to re-oil. Use a fine oil and use it sparingly. If you simply dip every moving part in a can of motor oil you will damage the finish on a wood stock and encourage particles to stick to all those oiled surfaces.

In the past I have used GI Weapons Oil, which is available on the surplus market at a reasonable cost. Shake hard before using to distribute the fine particles of Teflon, which always settle on the bottom. Do not use WD-40, which has little lubricating value and absolutely no staying power. Another negative of WD-40 is the way it creeps. Again, if it is sprayed near ammunition or into a magazine, it will quickly migrate into the cartridges, often destroying the powder and primer.

As mentioned earlier, if a contaminated cartridge is used and it manages to fire, it might only move its bullet an inch or two down the bore. If you failed to take notice of the weak report, the next bullet fired would hit the first, bulging the barrel. Curiously, this does not move both bullets out of the barrel; instead they are swaged together. Indeed, it is possible to fire bullet after bullet successively until the barrel is totally ruined and fully packed with solid lead. Often cartridges will burst in such a scenario, spraying shards of brass at high velocity out of the ejection port. If ever a report sounds unusually dull, or if there is no evidence that a bullet has left the barrel—always lock the bolt open, remove the magazine, and inspect the bore.

A stuck bullet will have to be removed with a stout rod and mallet. This should be done from the rear if possible. Often the barrel must be removed to facilitate this process. If two bullets are swaged together, a propane torch should be used to heat the barrel and melt the lead out. Be gentle with the torch and don't concentrate only on one area. Lead melts at around 625°F. If care is used, the barrel may not be damaged. As long as the bulge is not at the muzzle, accuracy may not be affected. New barrels are only $40 from the factory. Shooting glasses or safety glasses are always a good idea—especially if you shoot left-handed. So much for WD-40 and its use in a 10/22.

Lately I have taken to using bar and chain oil, formulated for use on the bar and chain of a chainsaw. This oil is moderately thick, has a very high lubricity, and tends to stay on moving surfaces. If you touch a drop with a finger and then pull away quickly, that drop will pull out into a thin strand a foot or two long, resembling a spider web. You can buy this oil wherever chainsaws are sold. Be sure to specify bar and chain oil, *not* two-cycle engine oil.

I put the oil into a small oilcan or a plastic squeeze container. A few drops go on the firing pin along the top of the bolt and are rubbed in with a fingertip. Another drop should go on the extractor, near the front of the bolt. I take the recoil spring assembly and apply about five drops to it, moving the operating handle back and forth a few times to make sure that the hole in the handle is well covered.

Next is the trigger group. You may be tempted to dip the entire unit in oil, but this is not a good idea. The first area is the hammer spring, and I put about three drops on the spring and one where the hammer strut turns inside the hammer.

Next is the hammer pivot pin, and I'll put a drop on each of the two bushings on the hammer. With the hammer cocked, I'll put a very large drop of oil on the sear area of the hammer. On older trigger groups this was difficult to do, but the newer trigger group castings have a hole on the right side, where one can both see and lubricate the sear area.

Next comes a drop on both sides of the main trigger pin, and a drop on the trigger plunger (in the trigger guard), where a spring returns the trigger to a forward position.

This done, I will cock and drop the hammer several times to work the oil in. I catch the hammer with my left thumb while pulling the trigger with my right finger so that the hammer never flies too far forward.

The last areas needing oil are the safety button, the pin for the magazine release button, and the magazine latch. These are all oiled sparingly and worked by hand to distribute the oil. Break Free is another lubricant with excellent lubricating properties.

If the firearm will be used in cold weather (say 0 to minus 60°F) most oils will stick and cause problems. You must use an oil specially formulated for cold temperatures. I have seen kerosene or Moly Dry Slide used in a pinch, and either certainly works better than no lubricant at all.

The first thing here is to install the recoil spring and the bolt. This is the most difficult part of the process, and many will not clean their

REASSEMBLY

Insert the hammer assembly into the trigger group.

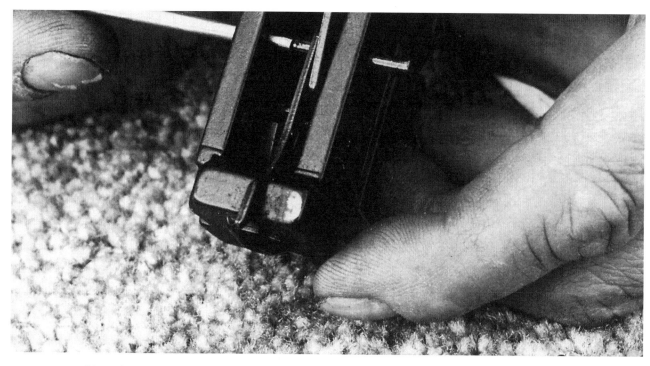

Move the pin ahead of the hammer to one side to allow the positioning of the bolt-stop spring
(on the right side of the hammer, with bent leg down).

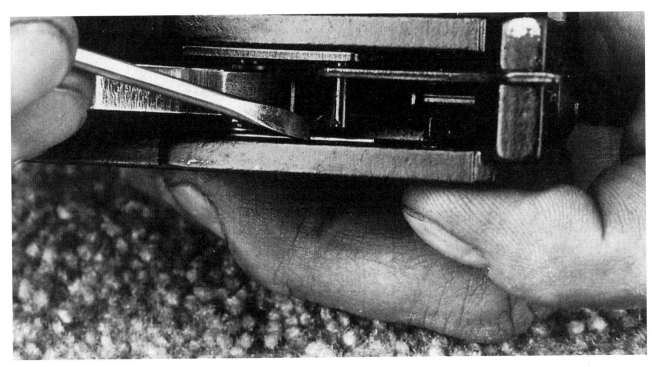

Push the spring on the right side of the hammer down with small screwdriver.
Hold the spring down and push the pin back over to keep it in place.
Remember, the smooth face of the hammer faces forward, and the bent leg of the spring goes down.

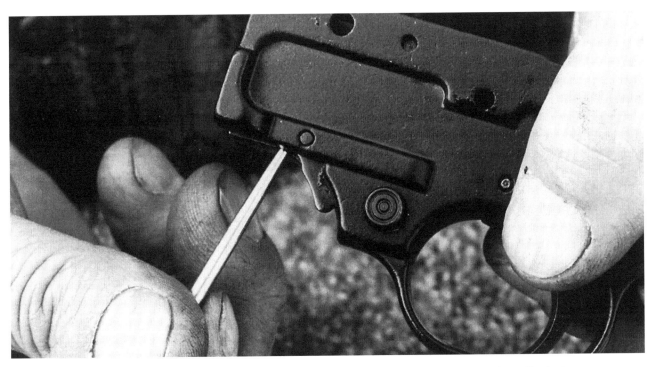

If the above step was performed properly, the bolt lock will work. Press up to release the lock.

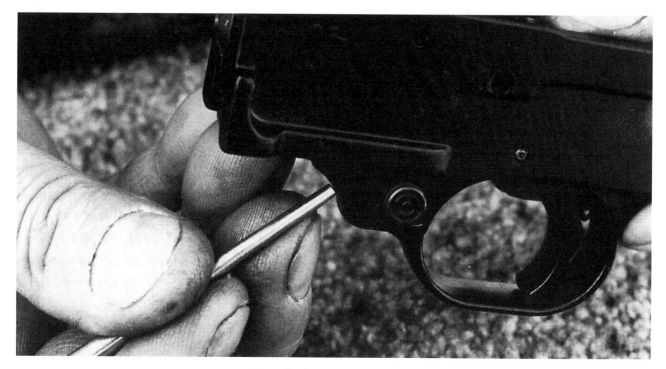

Press back to engage the lock.

Oil the hammer spring.

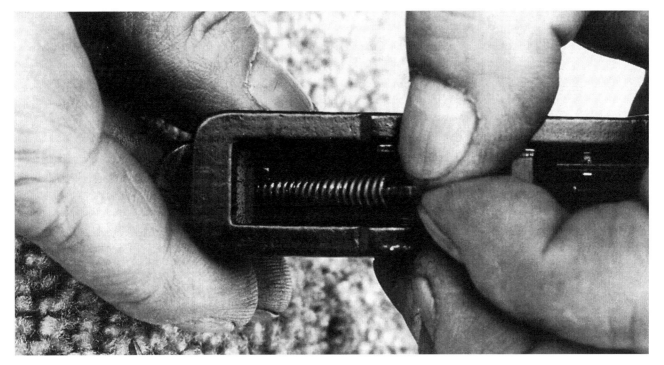

Insert the hammer spring and cock the hammer.

Insert the bolt return spring and compress it with screwdriver inserted through the ejection port.

Drop the bolt in place. Wiggle it until the charging handle fits into the bolt recess. The remainder of the reassembly procedure is easy and straightforward. Make sure the bolt lock is not engaged before reinserting the trigger group.

10/22s because of the hassle of getting the bolt in or out. Here's how to do it the easy way.

Firmly clamp the action, upside down, in a padded vise so that the ejection port is accessible and the barrel points toward you. Have the bolt and a medium-sized screwdriver positioned conveniently nearby.

Slide the recoil spring-rod-operating handle assembly into the ejection port and position the pointed end of the guide rod against the small recess provided at the rear of the receiver. The recess is small, and it is often difficult to hold the rod there while the spring is under tension. Another set of hands is often useful here. With the rod in place, move the operating handle to the rear to compress the spring. Unfortunately, the leverage on the handle binds against the rod (no matter how good the lubricant), so you are unable to do this using the part of the handle that extends beyond the receiver. I use a screwdriver or my left thumb, pressing against the operating handle but very close to the rod.

Once the spring is fully compressed, pinch the operating handle tightly to the receiver with your left thumb. The operating handle has a recess in the center, which will now be apparent. Put the blade of the screwdriver through the ejection port and into this recess. Hold the blade flat and at a 45-degree angle to the operating handle, pinching it down and pushing it firmly to the left side of the receiver. Drop the bolt into the receiver, so that its recess mates with the operating handle. Push the bolt down tightly against the op handle and then remove the screwdriver. Wiggle the bolt and the handle back and forth a few times. Eventually, the two will snap together and move under the restraining lip of metal near the ejection port.

You may achieve success the first time—but don't count on it. For many, this little chore is worth about 10 minutes of pain and aggravation. I can now do it in less than 10 seconds, and I no longer need a vise.

Once the bolt is in, I usually move it back

and forth to ensure that it is moving freely. I put either a drop of oil or a small drop of moly-filled wheel bearing grease on that area near the back and underside of the bolt where it contacts the hammer.

Take the barreled action out of the vise and drift the bolt retention pin into the receiver. Insert the trigger group (with the hammer cocked) and slide the rear pin into place. Sometimes the ejector (the piece of sheet metal that hits the rear of each shell as it is extracted) has moved from its groove and gets in the way. If this has happened, take the trigger group back out and move the ejector back to its proper position—facing the front of the action and sitting in its groove on the left side of the trigger group.

If the trigger group won't easily rotate down so that the front retention pin can be inserted, it means that the bolt-locking device (part #B-41) is sticking up. Draw the bolt all the way back, and the pin should go in. Don't force anything. The trigger group should go in easily.

Once together, cycle the bolt a few times to make sure that nothing is binding. Check the safety and drop the hammer to ensure that it and the trigger are functional. Problems encountered now won't disappear when the action has been fitted into the stock.

THE BOLT LOCK

The bolt lock may be released by retracting the bolt manually and pressing the lock up from below. You can set the lock by retracting the bolt and pressing the lock back. The bolt lock operates easily and well, once you get used to it.

As mentioned earlier, I always store, transport, and carry the 10/22 with the bolt locked open. I gain tremendous peace of mind from being able to glance at the weapon and know that it won't fire with its bolt locked open.

Older 10/22s have a problem with retaining their pins while the action is out of the stock. I wipe the receiver down (for oil) and use two small pieces of Scotch tape to cover one side of the receiver, over the three main pins. A zealot could cover both sides with tape, but this is rarely necessary.

Put the barreled action back into the stock (remember to put the safety into a central position) and insert the single action screw. Do not overtighten this screw. Look carefully at the barrel as you tighten the screw. If the barrel and action bend down into the stock the recess in the stock is too deep. It should be padded with one or more pieces of cardboard (from a cereal or ammunition box). Cut a small piece about an inch square and drill a 1/4-inch hole in its middle. Insert the shim over the action screw inside the stock. Keep adding shims until the barrel does not bend downward as the action screw is tightened. The barrel should float about 1/16 inch in the fore-end of the stock. More is too much; less is too little.

If your 10/22 has a barrel band, open it up a bit with a screwdriver before sliding it into place. Replace the scope, and the assembly is complete. The first time for this may take well over an hour. I can now do it in about 10 leisurely minutes. It is amazing how much better a 10/22 works when it is clean and properly oiled.

10/22 ACTION AND TRIGGER WORK

5

In the previous chapter we spent a lot of time dealing with disassembly and cleaning of the 10/22's action. Let us now assume we have a clean, empty 10/22 receiver attached to its barrel, and start from there.

DRILLING AN ACCESS HOLE FOR CLEANING THE BARREL

Over the past 10 years I have spent a lot of time and print preaching about the merits of a cleaning rod access hole in the rear of the 10/22's action. A number of those who work on the 10/22 now drill this hole. Perhaps the Ruger factory will do this someday—saving us all a lot of time and effort. In the meantime, here are two methods of accomplishing that end.

The method I currently employ involves machining a short piece of an older, worn-out 10/22 barrel. I use the rear end, which I cut to about 6 inches long. Part of the muzzle end of

that barrel has been turned to a parallel section on my lathe. That barrel stub is then clamped into a totally stripped receiver using the standard Ruger V-block and the two tensioning screws. The front of the barrel is then set into the three-jaw chuck on my lathe. This leaves the action able to spin in a motion parallel to the axis of the bore. With the tool post clear and the lathe turned on, I advance a center drill from the lathe's tailstock to spot the hole. I then advance a 7/32-inch drill in that same tailstock, drilling a hole through the back of the receiver. I deburr the hole with the twist of a countersink, and that completes the process. I should know better by now, but I am always pleasantly surprised when I squint through the hole and am able to see down the bore for the first time.

Some people are concerned about what would happen if a shell burst. Would some particles come back through the hole? In most cases, the rear hole is all but blocked out by the

Use a short dummy barrel in a lathe to centerdrill the rear action cleanout hole.

Use a 7/32-inch-diameter bit to drill the cleanout hole.

bolt-stop pin and then by the fact that it is buried in the stock. In addition, pieces of brass would have to get around the moving bolt, which is running interference. And a prudent person should be wearing shooting glasses. However, for those who are still concerned, it is easily possible to thread the access hole for 1/4-20 set screw. A 7/32-inch hole is the perfect size for 1/4-inch threads. You can then insert a 1/4-inch set screw, about 1/4 inch long, in the back of the receiver. This set screw could also be used to help hold the bolt-stop/buffer pin in place, although the battering it gets from the rear of the bolt would probably loosen that set screw in short order. If you want to thread the rear access hole, the perfect time is right after drilling it because the receiver is already clamped into position. You can simply put a 1/4-inch tap into the tailstock and turn the receiver by hand to make perfectly aligned threads. An aftermarket, fixed, plastic stock made by Butler Creek exposes the rear access hole, and a screw or plug should be used in conjunction with this stock.

For those without a lathe, there is another way to drill the rear access hole. It is still necessary to clamp a short stub of a worn barrel into the action. Buy a 3/16-inch extended drill about a foot long from a hardware store or a specialty shop. The drill may be chucked into an electric drill motor, thrust through the barrel stub, and used to drill the hole from the inside of the receiver. If you were going to drill a number of receivers it would be worth the effort to braze a 7/32-inch drill onto a section of 3/16-inch steel rod to make a slightly larger hole on the first pass.

As mentioned earlier, the rear access hole is useful for cleaning the 10/22's barrel from the breech. It not only allows this to be done with a fixed rod, it acts as a bore guide, so the chamber and throat will not be damaged. The hole is also useful for inspection and for bore-sighting the weapon.

MAKING THE ACTION QUIETER BY REPLACING THE STEEL BOLT BUFFER PIN

The slap of the steel bolt against the steel buffer pin can set up quite a racket. This is rarely noticed, however, because the noise of the muzzle report usually overshadows all else. In the case of a firearm using a sound suppressor, however, the clack of the bolt can become the dominant noise. Replacing the steel pin with a 1/4-inch-diameter nylon or polycarbonate pin helps to soften the noise of the recoiling bolt.

Some have attempted to soften the noise of the steel bolt's hitting the 10/22's barrel on the forward stroke. The most obvious solution is a heavy neoprene O-ring around the butt of the barrel. Progress has been made, but total success has not been achieved, the main problem being retention of the O-ring. Also, since the O-ring takes up space, that leaves less room for accumulated fouling.

A few quiet 10/22 users place a heavy cloth bag over the ejection port. This captures spent shells and dampens action noise to some degree. The bag inflates from gasses coming out the ejection port and keeps the passage free so that shells do not jam inside the port. The cloth bag is usually black and fairly flexible. Most that I have seen were professionally made and used a plastic clip to attach the bag over the opening. (Some missions require that all empty shell casings be retained, but this usually involves larger caliber weapons.) The bag must be quickly and easily removable in the event of a misfire or jam because it covers the bolt-operating handle.

WORKING ON THE BOLT AND THE FIRING PIN

Once the bolt is out and properly cleaned, the next step is to check the stroke of the firing pin. For this, you will need a straight edge, which can be anything from a machinist's steel rule to a Popsicle stick. Hold the bolt up to a good light source and hold the straight edge against the forward face of the bolt. Press the firing pin from the rear. We already know that the recess for the shell in the bolt face is .05 inch. For the best possible ignition, the stroke of the firing pin should allow the front of the pin to almost touch the straight edge. The design of most firing pins leads them to short-stroke, for to do otherwise would lead to impact between the firing pin and the barrel. This would, in turn, result in either a damaged firing pin or a damaged chamber—or both. The conservative design of all the pieces on the 10/22 leads to a firing pin with a stroke so short that it sometimes can't properly reach the .22's priming ring when the recess in the bolt face gets filled with waste from the firing process. This is what leads to misfires if ammunition with insensitive primers or unusually hard rims is encountered.

Russian primers are unusually hard to ignite, especially those in Baikal Jr. Steel and Jr. Brass cases. Although very accurate, this Russian ammunition is also very filthy; hence, it packs the recess in the bolt face and around the rear of the barrel quickly.

There are three main types of firing pin systems. The first is a pin, which is essentially a striker. This has its own driving spring and is released by a sear. It flies forward to strike its primer without any intermediary. The second employs a hammer to strike a pin, which flies forward to strike its primer. This second system uses the inertia of the pin as a safety mechanism: the pin is beyond the reach of the hammer when it is in contact with a primer. This is John Browning's design for the 1911 Colt .45 ACP pistol. The third system uses the firing pin as a direct link between hammer and primer because the hammer remains in direct contact with the rear of the pin when the front of that pin has contacted the primer. This last is the system used by Ruger in the 10/22.

The firing pin is a substantial piece of hardened sheet metal. It is restrained in its forward motion by a hardened-steel roll pin, which passes through an oval hole punched through the middle of the sheet-metal firing pin.

Ruger has made excellent use of hardened-steel components in the action. The hammer is harder than the firing pin. It is also harder than some 10/22 bolts. The rear face of the barrel is also hardened, and most are harder than the

average firing pin. The firing pin (part #B-11 for odering purposes) is one of the softer links in the chain. At a cost of $2.25, it is meant to fail before anything else. If yours has its rear face badly beaten by the hammer, it should probably be replaced.

Ruger had the good sense to know that his 10/22 carbines would be dry-fired millions of times by thousands of little boys who had run out of ammo. The oval hole in the center of the firing pin and the hardened steel roll pin are capable of absorbing a tremendous amount of punishment. If your firing pin fails to come close to the front surface of the bolt, the rear of that oval hole can be filed out a little. *Don't overdo this!* A few strokes are all it takes. If too much is taken out, the pin will strike the barrel and mess things up. If the pin projects beyond the front of the bolt, it should be replaced. I believe that the firing pin will achieve a greater velocity if the *front* of the hole is also enlarged a bit. By a bit, I mean no more than 1/16 inch.

The firing pin rests in a generous groove milled into the top of the bolt. The pin is loose in this groove, which is all to the good. If it were tight, oil adhesion would at times prevent it from moving fast enough to ignite a cartridge. Once the roll pin is driven out, the firing pin may be drawn to the rear to remove it. A very small, fairly stiff spring lies in the bottom of the groove in the bolt. This holds the firing pin to the rear, so that it stands proud of the bolt face—ready to be fairly struck by the hammer. I have disassembled a number of bolts that were missing this spring. The firing pin seemed to work fine without the spring, but I would rather have it than not. On newer weapons the tiny spring presses against yet another tiny pin driven into a blind hole in the side of the 10/22's bolt. Without side pressure from the spring, this pin often falls out of the bolt. One must watch for this—both spring and pin are easily lost.

Once the firing pin is out I usually take a moment to sand it lengthwise with a scrap of 220-grit sandpaper. This removes any burrs that are left after the stamping process. The earlier firing pins used to have a definite hook on the bottom face, where the spring pressed. The newer pins have no hook. While the pin is out of the bolt I use a small, round jeweler's file to restore the hook because I believe it helps to center the spring. Be sure that you don't accidentally sharpen the forward face of the firing pin. It must be square and dull to ignite the priming ring properly. A sharpened firing pin could actually pierce a cartridge—with unfortunate consequences.

THE EXTRACTOR

This is another part of the system that is often ignored. The extractor (part #B-14) will get worn or dull after about 50,000 rounds and should be replaced. This one part often fails at its task, and I've spent a lot of time trying to hook a spent casing out of the chamber with a pocket knife or a 2-inch nail. The extractor does not hinge on a pin but rather floats in a hole. Pushing the plunger to the rear a bit with a sharp scribe and then just pulling it straight out the side when the plunger clears may remove it. The extractor is the first thing to seize up and fail when the 10/22 is used around saltwater. I've seen entire rifles thrown in Dumpsters because their owners were tired of trying to make them work after a summer in salt spray.

THE BOLT

While the bolt is a replaceable part, I've never seen one worn out. The more expensive 10/22s have the face of the bolt that shows (but not the other side) nicely worked over and polished. I often take a moment to clean up the left side of the bolt with a few strokes of fine sandpaper, but there are other things that yield better results if cycling is a problem.

The lower rear face of the bolt contacts the hammer, which is the chief obstacle to the bolt as it recoils. Many think the .22 LR shell pushes rearward with considerable force. They are wrong. Initially, when the cartridge walls are under great pressure, they stick tightly to the sides of the chamber. Only when the pressure

drops substantially does the cartridge release its grip on the chamber walls. Then, the remaining pressure serves to push the spent shell and the bolt backward, so the self-cocking and self-loading process can begin anew.

If you primarily shoot high-energy, supersonic, high-speed, and ultravelocity cartridges in your 10/22, I recommend that you do nothing to your bolt. It should be fine as it is.

If you shoot only standard-velocity or subsonic ammo, you may experience cycling problems. If you have cycling problems there are two things that can be done to the bolt to resolve them. The first is to round and recontour the lower rear face of the bolt, so that it will more easily overpower the hammer in its rearward travel. I normally remove most of the material with a bench grinder. I then use a small, 1-inch, bench-mounted belt sander with a table to clean up the grinding marks. I make a sincere effort to get the rounded surface perfectly even, so that the hammer is pushed neither right nor left, but straight back. I don't take much material off, and I never grind into the horizontal groove on the back of the bolt, which affects the bolt-stop/recoil buffer pin.

With this complete, I'll take a little 220-grit sandpaper and hand-smooth the roughness created by the grinder.

It is also possible to drill one or two holes in the lower rear lobe of most bolts. If you do this, be sure that the firing pin and its spring have been removed first. The typical 10/22 bolt weighs about 6 ounces. Drilling one 3/8-inch hole in the rear lobe will reduce that weight to 5 1/2 ounces. Drilling a second 3/8-inch hole will result in a 5-ounce bolt. This allows faster cycling and more positive functioning with standard-velocity or subsonic ammunition. A hole in the rear of the bolt lobe will cause no problems. A hole in the forward part of the lobe may cause a problem with the firing pin spring, which will partially hang into space. A hook filed in the bottom of the firing pin may or may not correct this defect. Drill the forward hole at your own peril. A new bolt will cost about $25.

Round the rear of the bolt where it contacts the hammer. A grinder can be used to "hog" out the contour. A small belt sander will work to smooth out and true up the surface.

Smooth the surface further with a piece of sandpaper.

Buff the surface on a cloth wheel charged with rouge.

The lower bolt is unchanged. The upper one has been recontoured. There is no need to perform
this operation unless the weapon in question is having problems cycling standard-velocity or subsonic ammunition.

Some bolts are soft enough to drill to lighten them. This is recommended for short-barreled weapons or weapons that won't cycle fully because subsonic ammunition is being used.
Remove the firing pin for this operation.
Do not drill all the way through.

I used to drill the hole or holes all the way through the bolt, from left to right. Now I drill from the left side only, stopping just short of the right side. I use a short, 1/8-inch-diameter drill bit for a pilot hole. I then come in with a little cutting oil and a slow-turning 3/8-inch-diameter drill bit of cobalt tool steel. Afterwards I remove all burrs and carefully sand the modified bolt by hand. Some bolts are so hard that they can't be drilled.

Don't be tempted to use an EDM to lighten the bolt. An EDM is essentially a spark-erosion process that heats, quenches, and microhardens the heat-affected zone to the point that it is brittle and prone to cracking.

Again, don't alter the rear face of the bolt or try to drill the holes if cycling is not a problem.

An aftermarket bolt-operating handle and firing pin made of titanium may help cycling problems—or they may not. Titanium is roughly half the weight of steel, and a titanium firing pin may cut lock time a bit. Both the handle and the pin are fairly expensive. I have experienced numerous ignition failures with more than one brand of titanium firing pin. With regard to reliable ignition, I have had better luck with a stronger hammer spring on a factory firing pin.

THE 10/22 MACHINE GUN

Some police departments are using 10/22 rifles converted to full-auto fire (machine guns) as tactical entry weapons. The theory here is that .22 LR rounds may penetrate less and thus will be less likely to do peripheral damage than centerfire rounds. A short burst from a 10/22 machine gun would certainly be devastating because the converted firearms have a very high cyclic rate. I am not overly impressed with the ignition reliability of the .22 rimfire round, and this is a big concern with a tactical weapon. Only a few thousand legal 10/22 machine gun sears were registered before the 1986 ban. A few of these are in civilian hands. Police departments are free to purchase registered, full-auto sears manufactured at any time. I have fired a couple of

10/22 machine guns. They are extremely fast and very controllable. The barrels get hot, but not as hot as I would have expected.

THE HAMMER

We now move away from the receiver and into the trigger group. This module is very responsive to modification and is a joy to work on.

The 10/22's trigger pull is largely dependent upon the angle of the sear and depth of engagement of the sear in the hammer. You need never take the trigger out of the group. The work can all be done at the hammer.

At this time I should mention that if you ever do take the trigger out of the group, you will probably have a very tough time getting it back in properly. A useful hint here is to cut a short section of toothpick or piece of the thin tube on a can of carburetor cleaner. This piece should be no longer than the widest section in the trigger assembly and can be used to hold that assembly together while it is worked down into the action. Once the trigger is in position, the real pin can be pushed into place, displacing the temporary pin. Again, avoid taking the trigger out of the group if at all possible.

To remove the hammer, proceed as follows. Push the safety button to the off position. Pull the trigger to release the hammer all the way forward. Push the hammer spring out from the bottom with a small probe or a #8 nail. Now, push the hammer's pivot pin out of the left side of the group. Pause for a moment and note the position of the spring on the *right* side of the hammer. The bushings in the hammer are identical, but the spring always goes on the *right side of the hammer*, with the bent leg on the bottom. Remove the spring and the bushings.

Look at the hammer and note the depth of the sear notch on the bottom. The angle of the sear face causes the hammer to be cocked a little more when the trigger is pulled. If you slack off on the trigger, pressure from the hammer spring causes the hammer to engage the sear more fully.

This is as it should be. Do not touch the angled interior face of the sear. Most of the work on reducing the trigger pull can be done by removing some of the sear material, thus reducing the depth of engagement. Since the hammer is usually quite hard, using a file will not normally be possible, even though a file would otherwise be the ideal tool here because it offers the perfect amount of control and metal removal. Some 10/22 hammers are soft enough to file, but I rarely see one.

At this point I must mention that removing the proper amount of metal from the sear is not an easy task, and it is one that is best left to a professional gunsmith. If too much material is taken off, the hammer will release too easily and the safety will not function. This is a very dangerous situation. If you attempt to perform this job without the necessary skill and judgment, you could easily ruin the hammer. If this happens, the only option is to buy and install another hammer from Ruger (Part #B-17) for $5 and throw the ruined one away.

A hammer without adequate sear engagement will not catch on the return stroke. It could commence to fire automatically and not stop until the magazine is empty. This, too, is dangerous, and the only remedy is to replace the hammer. Possession of an unregistered, untaxed machine gun is a serious federal felony, and machine guns are banned in about a third of the 50 states.

Many companies now offer aftermarket hammers made either of steel or titanium. These hammers have sears that are carefully stoned and will produce a pull of about 3 pounds. They are fairly expensive.

One thing you can do to improve the function of the hammer is to lightly sand the forward face, where it contacts the bolt. This should be done by hand, using longitudinal strokes. Both this area and the sear area of the hammer may then be buffed on a cloth buffing wheel using fine jeweler's rouge. Don't overdo the buffing. You want the surfaces slick, but not so slick that they won't hold lubricant.

If the trigger pull is too heavy, the hammer sear can be stoned. Do not remove any metal from inside the notch. Do not overdo the stoning procedure, or an unsafe condition may result.

Sand the forward face of the hammer where it contacts the bolt and then polish lightly on a buffing wheel.

THE TRIGGER

As mentioned earlier, I do not recommend taking the trigger out of the group. If work on the hammer went well, the trigger should pull from 3 to 4 pounds before the sear trips. A number of firms sell trigger scales, and I measure and record every trigger (hammer) I work on. One thing that will reduce the apparent pull is to install a trigger shoe. This covers the existing trigger face, widening it to increase surface area. This can cut the apparent pull significantly.

THE TRIGGER STOP
OR OVERTRAVEL LIMIT

As each shot is discharged, the trigger will usually move beyond the point where the hammer was released. This excess movement causes the firearm to move a bit, throwing the shot. It is possible to halt trigger movement after the point of release. This results in a considerable increase in field accuracy. A low-tech method of installing a stop would be to put a 1/16-inch-long section of weed whacker trim cord or a tiny nylon ball inside the spring that holds the trigger forward. This is very tough to fit and requires that both trigger and hammer be removed a number of times before the fit is perfect. I did this on a couple of 10/22s before I went to a conventional set screw.

I now use a 6-40 set screw about 3/8 inch long. This is installed through the back of the trigger guard. I carefully center-punch the rear of the trigger guard, and drill a .103-inch-diameter hole. I tap this hole, trying to aim the tap so that it will contact the center of the back of the trigger. I then put a drop of red Loctite on the screw and run it in and out until the trigger only moves about .003 inch after it drops the hammer. Less travel will bind the trigger, increasing the pull. More travel will cause finger movement. The Loctite will set up in about an hour.

Others take the trigger out and install a 4-40 screw through the face of the trigger. This

Center-punch for the trigger-stop screw using a spring-loaded tool.

Drill the hole using a 1/8-inch-diameter bit.

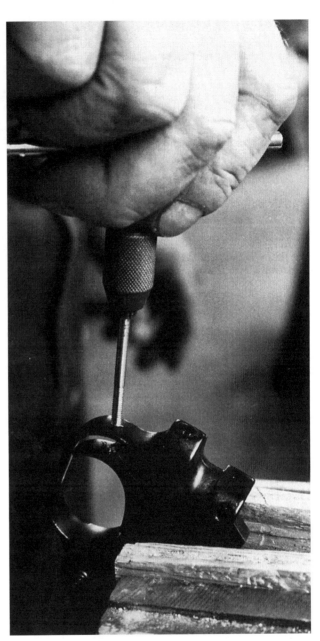

Tap the hole with a 6-40 bottoming tap.

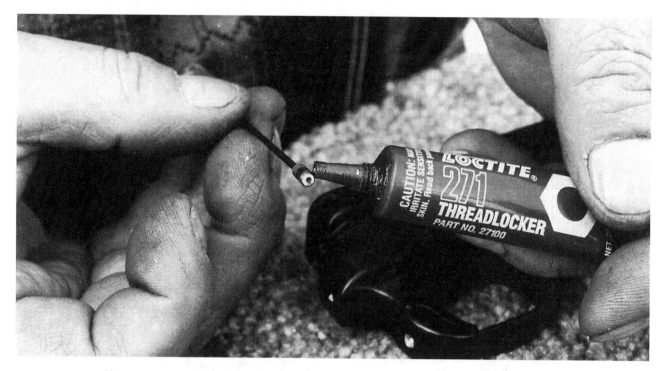

Use a 6-40 set screw between 1/4 and 3/8 inch long. Put a drop of Loctite on the screw.
Adjust in and out until the hammer is released with a trigger pull, but ensure that the trigger doesn't move rearward excessively.
Back off an additional 1/4 turn to ensure freedom of movement. Allow Loctite to set up.

accomplishes the same end and looks neater but seriously weakens the soft, cast-aluminum trigger. An excited hunter could forget to remove the safety in the heat of the night, pull too hard, and snap the trigger right off at the screw.

The overtravel screw does about as much good as a lighter trigger. If I had to choose one over the other, I would opt for the screw because it has absolutely no effect on safety, whereas a very light trigger may be detrimental to safety.

I recently did a two-stage trigger for a friend. The sear face (which I never touch) had a little bump in it, which made the trigger function like a two-stage military trigger. This worked out very well: he could take up on the trigger until a little click could be felt; at this point, he could adjust the aim slightly. When the sight picture was perfect, another ounce of pressure released the hammer.

THE HAMMER STRUT

Take the hammer strut and clamp the rounded end in a vise. Press the spring down and pull the retainer off, noting the position that it was in. Remove the spring. Lightly sand the four corners of the straight shaft of the strut in a lengthwise direction. Buff the corners to make them smooth. Lightly stone the rounded end of the strut, where it will enter and rotate on the hammer. Reinstall the spring and the keeper. This should reduce internal friction by a small amount, allowing the hammer to hit a little harder. A stronger hammer spring is available through Brownells if you feel that you need it. You should only use the stronger spring if you experience misfires and have done everything else possible to eliminate them.

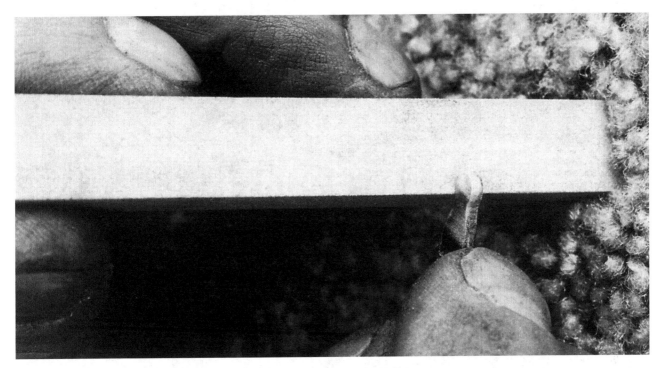

Lightly stone the surfaces of the hammer strut where they engage the hammer.

REINSTALLING THE HAMMER

Reinstall the bushings in the lower hole in the hammer and place the spring on the right side with the bent end down. Remember that the smooth face of the hammer should be forward. Insert the hammer assembly into the trigger group. Pull the trigger to reduce pressure on the hammer while looking through the hole for the hammer's pin. When the hammer bushings line up, thrust the pin into place to fasten it all together.

Now for the toughest part—the side spring. There is a pin in the trigger group casting forward of the hammer. Push this pin from the right until it is about halfway out, leaving a gap on the right side of the cavity in the trigger group. Rotate the side spring all the way forward. Take a small screwdriver and compress the upper leg of that spring, pinching it against the right side of the inside of the housing for the trigger group, until that leg is forced beneath the hole for the pin. As soon as that occurs, quickly push the pin back into position from the left. That job done, rotate the hammer all the way forward. Pull the trigger (if necessary) to allow that to occur. Insert the hammer spring (keeper first) into the hole in the rear of the receiver. Feed the top of the hammer strut into the slot in the back of the hammer. Cock the hammer. The job is done!

Lubricate and test according to instructions in the previous chapter on disassembly, cleaning, and reassembly.

MAGAZINE INSERTION AND REMOVAL

One of the inherent problems with the 10/22's magazine is that it is difficult to insert easily. It is even more difficult to claw it out of its socket for removal, since there is no convenient handle to grab. A small bevel on the centering hole in the forward part of the receiver will ease insertion and removal. I use a small, sharp Sloyd knife to make this bevel. Do not overdo this operation.

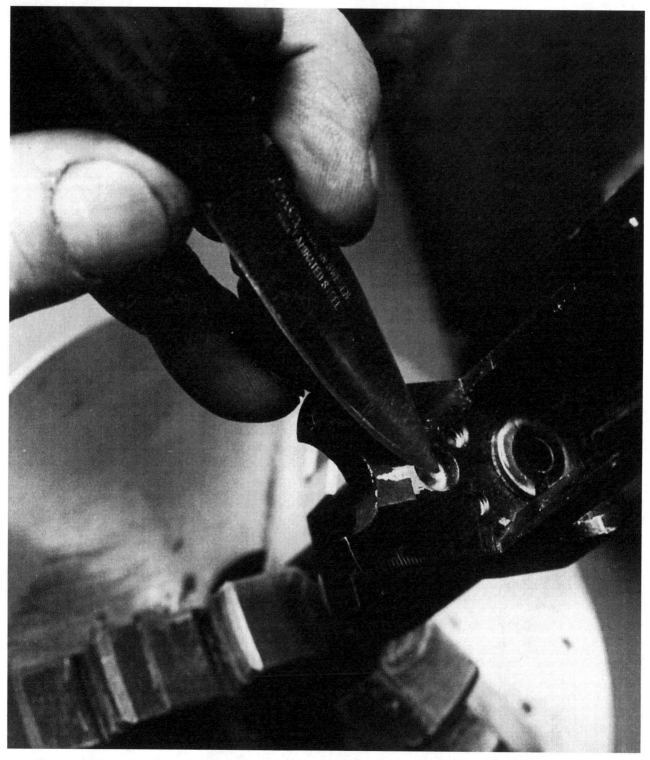

A small knife can be used to round the lip on the catch that holds the magazine in place.
This will aid in magazine insertion and removal.

IRON SIGHTS AND SCOPES

6

IRON SIGHTS

The existing front sight on the typical 10/22 is strong, visible, and fairly effective for short-range work. It consists of a small brass bead atop a tapered post. Wear usually keeps the bead bright. This makes it easily seen and rapidly acquired in the typical low-light conditions often found in a forest environment. In bright light, however, the brass bead shines brilliantly, making precise aim difficult.

According to rifle guru Jeff Cooper, the brass bead is not as precise as a thin post. It is possible to make the existing front sight into a tapered post by filing off the bead. It is also possible to order another post front sight to replace the existing one. A common front sight adjustment places the brass bead directly over the area where the bullet will hit. With a post, the impact area is usually placed just above the top of the post. This

allows somewhat more precise shot placement in both the horizontal and vertical directions. This is not recommended for a rifle that will be used in varying and low light conditions. If the rifle will be used for hunting at dusk, I recommend that the existing front sight not be changed.

The rear sight consists of a U-shaped notch with a white diamond below. The white diamond is very useful in low-light conditions. The notch is not precise, although one can acquire it quickly for close-range use. At least one aftermarket vendor sells a replacement peep sight insert for the rear sight. The peep sight automatically centers the eye's pupil in the hole. The rear insert is held in place with extremely small screws, which, when loosened, permit a small amount of adjustment. The factory rear sight is spring loaded and will fold forward to make room for a scope or a receiver-mounted peep sight.

SIGHT CORRECTION

The original rear sight can be adjusted to some degree by loosening the microscopic screws in the rear and moving the sight leaf in the direction you want the new bullet flight pattern to go. For instance, if the group tends to shoot left, drift the entire rear sight to the right a bit by driving it in its groove in the barrel in that direction. If the rifle tends to shoot low, loosen the tiny screws and move the leaf upward to compensate. There is very limited adjustment in the factory sight. If you are confused about direction, exaggerate the proposed movement in your mind. That is, mentally raise the sight a foot and then see where the bullets will be directed. For some reason it is often confusing which way the sight should be moved to effect the proper change.

Again, the rear sight should be moved in the direction you want the bullets to go. The front sight should be moved *opposite* the desired change. Raising the rear sight will raise the impact point. Filing a bit off the top of the front sight will effectively lower that front sight, which will also raise the impact.

For target work, the brass bead on the front sight may be cut off, leaving a very thin, sharp post. This is more precise for shooting at a mark on paper. In this case, the rear sight would be folded down and an aftermarket peep sight installed on the receiver. The least expensive rear peep is made by Williams and is adjustable for a fixed distance. It cannot be readily adjusted for use in long-distance target work or for conditions where a temporary crosswind exists. Adjustable rear aperture (peep) target sights are available, but they can easily cost more than the basic 10/22 rifle.

Extensive testing of iron sights by the United States during World War II led to the adoption of the parallel front post combined with a rear peep sight. These components are inexpensive, effective, and durable. For a simple sighting system in field use or for a compact survival weapon, this system is hard to beat. It is vastly superior to the V- or U-shaped notch common on firearms built in the 1800s.

OPTICAL SIGHTING SYSTEMS

Scopes came into development before the Civil War, in the 1850s. Market pressure and increased manufacturing ability after World War II have steadily improved the offering and decreased the price. Weaver first came out with his inexpensive B-4 and B-6 .22 LR scopes in the 1960s. These had tiny, 3/4-inch-diameter steel barrels and equally tiny objective lenses. Inexpensive though they were, they proved durable and far more accurate than most factory iron sights.

The market and supply of optical systems have burgeoned in recent years, and an incredibly wide variety of scopes is now available. For general field use I recommend a standard 4 to 6x scope with a 1-inch-diameter barrel and an objective lens at least 30mm (1.2 inches) in diameter. These are inexpensive, usually trouble free, and will serve the intended purpose well. A number of brands are available. Some I have been happy with include Leupold, Redfield, Simmons, Swift, and Tasco. Most carry a limited lifetime warranty. A survival rifle would be well equipped with a small 2 to 2.5x compact scope with a 20mm objective lens, such those made by Simmons.

As we move up the ladder of quality and expense, Tasco makes a scope called the Big Horn that has brilliant optics. This scope is roughly 3 inches in diameter (with lens covers) and 13 inches long. It belongs on the more accurate and expensive Ruger 10/22T target model with its heavy, laminated stock and hammer-forged barrel. The Big Horn is a 2.5 to 10x variable with a huge 50mm (2-inch) objective lens, a 1-inch barrel, and a range focus adjustment on the front objective bell. The 50mm lens gathers a tremendous amount of light at dusk, allowing you to see fairly well if the power ring is turned to the middle range. Typically, you adjust the focus at the rear to accommodate your individual eye prescription. If others use the same scope they will either have to suffer with a blurred, eye-pulling image or individually adjust the rear lens to accommodate their eye, leaving the system maladjusted for the original user. With the Tasco Big Horn the necessary adjustment can be taken care of with a simple twist of a large ring on the front objective lens. You can also use that adjustment feature to accommodate for ranges between 6 yards and infinity. Since much of the enjoyment of plinking at inanimate objects comes from seeing the bullets strike, the quality of the image enhances the enjoyment. The image quality of the Tasco Big Horn is superb. It has a retail price ranging from $250 to $400.

As we continue to move up the ladder of quality and expense, Tasco also makes a scope called the World Class Plus (WCP). This scope also has a 50mm objective (front) lens and a 1-inch barrel. It has very fine crosshairs and a tiny target dot in the center of the reticle. It has a front focus ring, external elevation and windage knobs, and variable power between 8 and 32x. This is a scope that would be useful in benchrest target shooting and BR 50 matches. Measuring between 15 and 21 inches in length (depending on whether one or two sunshades are added), it would not be a good hunting scope because it would take too long to acquire a target. Like those on the Big Horn, the WCP's optics are brilliant. Unlike the Big Horn, which has plastic scope covers held on with elastic, the WCP scope has opaque, screw-on lens covers made of aluminum. These take a while to remove, and a mild blow during handling could dent them, which may present a real problem. The retail prices for this scope range from $300 to $450, depending on the source.

Both the Big Horn and the WCP scopes require rings that are extra, extra high to allow the front objective bell to clear the barrel. Even this may not provide the required clearance, and I have at times had to pad the area beneath the mounting rings with strips of card stock to get the necessary relief.

As we get near the top of the price ladder, we have the Bausch & Lomb Elite 3000. This has a 30mm barrel, and a 50mm objective lens, is variable between 3 to 9x, and has an easily rotated focus ring on the rear objective bell. This scope is 3 inches in diameter and about 16 inches long. It may be tougher than the Tasco offerings, and it has fewer bells and whistles. It is a quality scope with a price tag hovering around $500. Its optics are not more brilliant than either of the Tascos previously mentioned, although it has been rated an excellent buy by anyone who has ever used one. It comes with a standard duplex reticle or a European hunting reticle with very broad outer crosshairs on the bottom and both sides. Bausch & Lomb also offers an Elite 4000 for a little more money. This scope differs in that it comes with a sunshade or two, has a smaller 1-inch tube, has range focus on the forward lens bell, and is variable between 6 and 16x. With a thinner barrel and more moving parts, the Elite 4000 may not be as tough or as weatherproof as the Elite 3000.

Most people never take their rifles out during damp or rainy weather; hence, the integrity of the scope's envelope is never truly tested. A variable-power scope may not fog up during rainy weather, but the chances that it will are greater. If your 10/22 rifle will be used in wet weather I still recommend a fixed 4x scope. Leupold seems to have the best reputation for not fogging in bad weather. There are hundreds of types and brands of scopes available. I have only mentioned those that I feel are a good buy and that I have had personal experience with. Spending more money will not necessarily buy a better optic. It is best to ask around before settling on a particular brand or model.

SCOPE-MOUNTING SYSTEMS

The factory Ruger 10/22 comes with a tiny aluminum strip that acts as a base for mounting a set of .22 LR rings with 3/8-inch claws. Unfortunately, this strip is inadequately sized for the pounding the action takes as the bolt slams against the barrel and rear stop. Very few small rings will stand up to the pounding, so I do not recommend that this base be used, even though it comes free of charge.

The Weaver mounting rail has become standard in the United States, and it consists of an extruded section of aluminum, to which rings with 1-inch claws attach. Often there are slots in these 1-inch bases, and the slots accommodate transverse mounting screws for the rings. The screws bind in the slots and prevent the scope from moving forward or backward in reaction to the bolt slamming repeatedly against the barrel. Since the patents ran out on the rail system years ago, a great many manufacturers now build mounting bases and rings to fit them.

For a permanent mount, I recommend securing a proper base to the top of the 10/22 action with both epoxy and the four screws provided. Put a small dab of grease or oil in each screw hole: the day may come when you want to take the mounting rail off the action. If the threads of the screws are epoxied into place it is possible to strip the heads, especially if Allen screws are used. Take care to ensure that the screws are not too long by cycling the action after each screw is snugged into place. If a screw binds against the bolt, it will have to be removed and the end ground down until it no longer binds. This is not an aspect to be ignored. It will create a function problem that will not go away.

The rings I like most are those that are vertically split. One manufacturer of this type of rings is Custom Quality Products in Madison Heights, Michigan. These rings are cut from quality extrusions and are held in place with screws that are a little larger and stronger than most. They are made for both 1-inch and 30mm scope barrels. The one for a 1-inch barrel will accommodate a front objective bell with an OD of almost 2 inches (or an inside lens of 44mm) over a heavy target barrel. Most extruded aluminum rings are not very expensive, frequently less than half what steel rings cost. The scopes with large objective bells may require expensive rings with more extension. As optics get less expensive, we will eventually see 60 to 80mm objective lenses become commonplace.

If you will want to remove the scope frequently, a style of ring called the tip-off is required. These are not normally as secure and are held in place with a bent metal clip instead of a claw on one side. They come in handy if you want to dip the action in solvent during the cleaning process—it would not do to dip a scope in solvent. Again, the rings I've had the least trouble with are Custom Quality Products' vertically split ones, although those made by Tasco and others are certainly adequate. Tasco supplies a rail and rings in one convenient package, and the rail it distributes is very well made.

AFTERMARKET STOCKS

7

The folks at Ruger have seen the wave of the future and currently produce at least four factory stocks for the 10/22: birch, walnut, black plastic, and laminated wood.

The factory mainstay, which is made of birch, is the most common. (As this book goes to press, the world's supply of wood appears to be dwindling, and Ruger is now supplying its models with plastic stocks at a lower price than those made of other materials.) It carries the cast-aluminum barrel band, a Ruger trademark and cosmetic design feature that has helped sell a lot of rifles. Although the barrel band would provide a measure of strength if the rifle were to be used with a bayonet in battle, it usually decreases accuracy. A holdover from the 15th century, this band is a feature that should be allowed to die a natural death. The factory buttplate is slick plastic that won't hold still on the shoulder.

The deluxe 10/22 carries a nicely finished walnut stock with checkering, a rubber buttplate, and an adequate forearm without a barrel band.

Although it costs more, this stock makes the 10/22 a very fine weapon for use in target shooting, hunting, plinking, and field activities where abuse won't be severe. This is the stock I would use for most activities and is the one I recommend.

The factory 10/22 stock is made of black plastic with a smooth, pleasant texture (unfortunately, it retains the cast-aluminum barrel band of the original). Both checkering and the buttplate are cast in place. This stock is attractive, tough, and fairly comfortable. If abuse or wet weather is likely, I would choose this stock in combination with a stainless barrel. If you are starting from square one, it is usually less expensive to buy a firearm in a factory configuration closest to what is needed, instead of buying what is closest to hand, and adding to that.

The last stock is reserved for Ruger's heavy target (T) models, which are available with either stainless- or blued-steel barrels. This stock is made of heavy laminated wood and is designed to be used with a scope. It has a rubber buttplate and is moderately comfortable to use off a bench. The weight of the weapon precludes use in the field, but it would be suitable for varmint and target shooting.

Almost all of Ruger's factory stocks have the recess (where the single bearing point of the action lies) cut too deeply. Hence, almost all of the stocks cause the barrel to be bent when the action screw is tightened. The cure for this problem lies in a shim, about an inch square, cut from thin cardboard or gasket material. One or more shims are placed under the action bearing point, where the single screw ties the stock to the action. I usually keep inserting shims until the barrel no longer bends when the action screw is tightened. Bedding with Bondo or Marinetex is also a solution, but the cardboard shims are faster and almost as effective.

AFTERMARKET STOCKS

Aftermarket stocks are offered by a variety of manufacturers, with new ones entering the market almost monthly.

Wooden stocks, while appealing from a traditional point of view, are dinosaurs. From a production standpoint they take a lot of time to manufacture and finish, and, therefore, are going to be more costly to produce as time goes by. Wooden stocks show wear and scratches in use, are a bit heavier than necessary, and usually cause shifts in impact because of moisture lost or absorbed in response to weather variations.

Injection-molded plastic stocks have a high molding cost, but once the tooling is done, they can be produced inexpensively at the rate of one per minute, with little or no finishing required. Plastic stocks are fairly lightweight and durable, show little in the way of wear, and are affected very little by rain and humidity—though some become brittle in extremely cold temperatures.

Some plastic stocks are hand-built in open molds. These tend to be a little lighter, more stable, and very expensive. They may cost three or four times what a factory 10/22 costs.

Wooden stock manufacturers are trying to cope with the change but are having a hard time surviving. In fact, several have gone into bankruptcy.

Fajen laminated stocks are occasionally available. They are quite handsome, fairly to moderately heavy, and offer some interesting and unusual shapes. One nice thing about the wooden stock is that a master blank can be fabricated at modest cost, and tracer lathes can be used to produce duplicate shapes at a modest cost. Sanding and finishing are time consuming and expensive when compared with injection-molded plastic.

Butler Creek offers both fixed and folding stocks for the 10/22. These are nicely designed, lightweight, durable, and accurate. Butler Creek also offers combination packages with a stock and an aftermarket replacement barrel at an attractive price. The deluxe stock has a pebbled-surface finish that looks good and absorbs wear better. It is worth spending the extra money on the deluxe finish.

Choate Manufacturing is the acknowledged king of the plastic stock. Choate offers a good, basic midline stock that is durable and utilitarian at a fair price. Some people really like the ergonomics of Choate's Dragunov-style 10/22 stock, while others find it uncomfortable. Standard pull length (distance from butt to trigger face) is 13.5 inches in the United States. Choate offers its stock with a pull starting at 14 inches, with spacers available to increase that pull to at least 16 inches. This is good for large men but does little for youths and small-framed men and women. The stock would be better with a pull starting at 11 inches.

Hogue offers an interesting stock with a fiberglass core and a rubber coating over the entire surface. These are grippy and handle abuse well, but dirt seems to stick to the surfaces with tenacity. Only one length of pull is offered. Combination barrel/stock packages are offered.

McMillan offers one or two high-end stocks. These are lightweight, moderately strong, accurate, and very expensive. Some like the ergonomics, and others don't.

HS Precision also offers high-end 10/22 thumbhole stocks. An added feature is the rear cast-off for right-handers, where the butt curves to the right (it appears to be crooked when viewed from the top) by about 1/2 inch. This aids comfort and accuracy. The stock is lightweight, rigid, accurate, and very expensive. All aftermarket stocks come with sling swivel attachment points for a shooting sling.

This excellent factory Ruger synthetic stock has been shortened to get rid of the barrel band and to accommodate a long muzzle can welded to a short barrel. Synthetic material was used in place of wood because birch is becoming scarce. Photo by Al Paulson

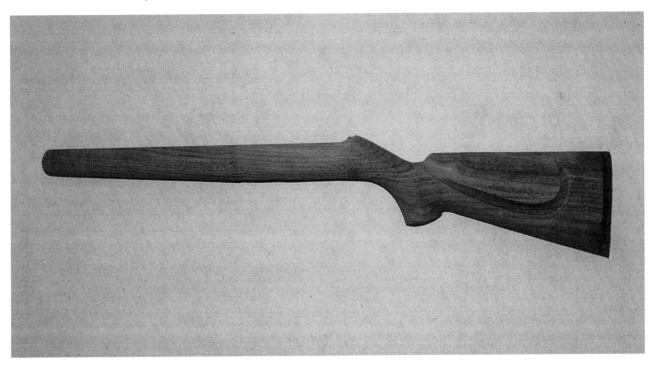

Premilled stock blank, ready for sanding and finishing. Photo by Mark White

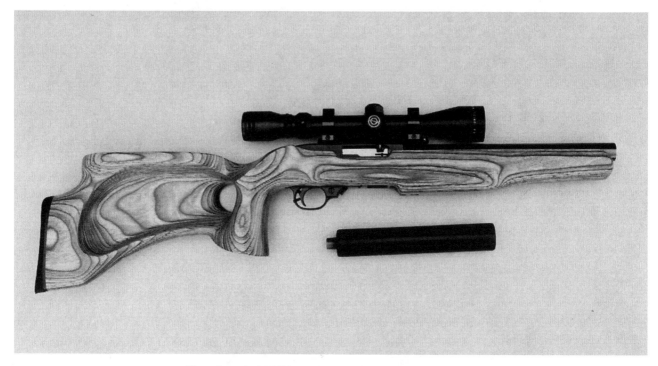

Short-barreled 10/22 mounted in Fajen silhouette stock.
The Sound Tech Millennium Can has been removed. Photo by Al Paulson

Factory Ruger stock on top; chopped Butler Creek stock below. Photo by Mark White

Registered short-barreled rifle with high-volume, 7-inch Sound Tech can, mounted in chopped Choate folding stock. This weapon is only 18 inches long when folded and weighs 6 pounds with bipod and scope. Photo by Al Paulson

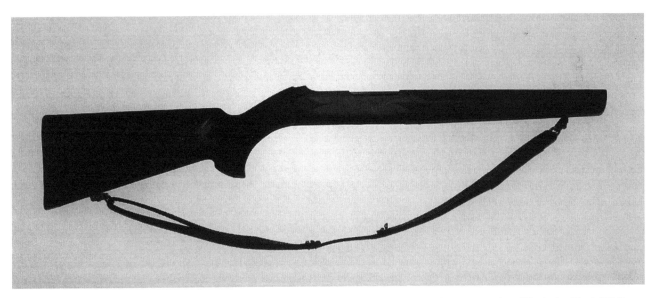

Hogue fiberglass stock over molded with soft rubber—a good stock for hunting in wet weather. Photo by Mark White

Ugly but functional, this metal stock is fashioned of welded aluminum and weighs only 11 ounces. Photo by Mark White

BUILDING A SIMPLE 10/22 SILENCER

8

In the late 1980s we manufactured an inexpensive 10/22 silencer that was fairly effective with subsonic ammunition. Its plans are included here for those who live in countries where silencers are not restricted and for those in the United States who have the time, money, and persistence to deal with the $200 federal tax; Bureau of Alcohol, Tobacco, and Firearms (BATF) Form 1; and fingerprint cards required. Please note that in the United States the forms must be filled out, filed, and returned, and the $200 tax must be paid before the silencer is constructed. A metal lathe will probably be required.

CONSTRUCTION

Begin by removing the factory 10/22 barrel from its action or start with a nontapered, aftermarket, blued, bull barrel. If one is using the 18 1/2-inch tapered factory barrel, it should be cut to 16 1/4 inches in length. It will have to be built up with a piece of bar stock and turned between centers because of its tapered profile, which is hard to grab in a three-jawed chuck. We will be using a parallel 18- or 21-inch aftermarket barrel (cut to 16 1/2 inches) for illustration purposes.

The tube or body of the silencer is the registered, numbered part in the United States. A piece of 4130 chrome-moly steel tubing can be purchased from Aircraft Spruce and Specialty Co. Quite a number of options are available with regard to tubing length and diameter. Prospective silencer builders are advised to weigh their options carefully.

In the late 1980s we made up quite a number of different styles, lengths, and diameters of experimental 10/22 silencers, all of which were fused to their dedicated barrels with weld or soft solder. After an intensive testing program we were surprised to learn that a simple 1 x 7-inch tube with a single flat baffle and two pieces of rolled mesh was among the most successful of the designs. An effective silencer will often defy computer analysis. Cut-and-try procedures can be more effective in some applications.

To begin, obtain an 8-inch-long piece of 1-inch-OD 4130 seamless-steel tubing with a .049-inch wall thickness. Be advised that Aircraft Spruce will sell only materials in even 1-foot increments. Most other suppliers only sell in 20-foot lengths and have minimum orders of $1,000. Steel tubing is available in wall thicknesses of .035, .049, .058, and .065. I chose .049 because it will slip over the outside of a heavy 10/22 barrel with a minimum of machine work.

The tube should be held in the three-jawed chuck of a metal lathe, and the ends should be faced off square and clean. A triangular deburring tool should be manually held inside one end of the spinning tube to remove any burrs that exist and scrape the inside of the tube clean for about an inch in depth. The inside diameter should be carefully measured with vernier calipers. The tube will fit over the muzzle end of the heavy 10/22 barrel for about an inch. Put the barrel in the lathe and turn about an inch of the muzzle end down to the inside diameter (ID) of the tube, which should be about .920 inch. Take two or three very light cuts with a sharp bit to recrown the muzzle. If the ID of the tube turns out to be .902 inch, for instance, it would be permissible to turn the OD of the barrel step down to .901 inch, which would leave .001 inch clearance between the barrel and tube when one is slipped over the other. Be careful not to take too much material off. If the fit of the barrel to the tube is sloppy, the barrel's diameter can be increased a trifle with a knurling tool. If I have only .001 inch to remove, I will often do it with a stroke of a file to get the fit just right.

Once the fit is perfect, the tube can be bonded to the barrel with a couple of drops of Red Loctite or soft 50-50 lead-tin electrical solder. A novice will probably get the best result with Red Loctite or Two-Ton epoxy as an adhesive. An experienced machinist will do a better job by soldering the joint with a propane torch. Soldering takes skill but will yield a longer lasting joint. Plain steel solders very easily and well; stainless steel does not. If the fit is a bit tight, the tube can be forced into place with a bar clamp of the type used in woodworking. Spin the barrel in the lathe. If the alignment of the tube is perfect it will spin without wobbling.

The primary expansion chamber is about 3 1/2-inches long and will be filled with a 3 1/2-inch-long section of tightly wound mesh or 1/8-inch-square galvanized hardware cloth. This material can be purchased at a hardware store or home center. Do not substitute 1/4-inch mesh. Using a pair of tin snips, cut a section of 1/8-inch mesh about 18 inches long and 3 1/2 inches wide. Use a section of 3/8-inch-diameter wooden dowel or 5/16-inch bolt as a mandrel to wind the mesh around. I usually pull two short strands from the mesh with a small set of pliers. This leaves 1/4-inch-long strands on the 3 1/2-inch-wide end, which are tucked into the weave and bent over to keep them from unraveling. Stray wires have a way of loosening and sticking up into the bullet's path. Some who do this even go so far as to solder the first wrap of mesh down with a soldering iron and electrical solder. Wind the rest of the strip around the mandrel as tightly and evenly as possible. Remove the mandrel and push the coil of mesh into the tube. The coil must be kept tight, and its center should be aligned in the tube to match with the center of the bore. There is plenty of clearance with the center, so the fit doesn't have to be perfect. If the coil won't fit, cut a wrap or two off. If it is too loose, cut a longer section. The coil of mesh should nest tightly against the barrel in the bottom of the tube. Some use a tight wrap of electrical tape over the coil to hold it together until it goes into the tube. A short length of dowel can be used to drive the mesh all the way in.

Do not use copper, bronze, or aluminum window screen for this component because it won't hold up. Galvanized- or soldered-steel hardware cloth works well because the lead or zinc coating doesn't react with the lead vapor and acids accompanying each charge of propellant gas. A heavy, woven stainless-steel screen will work, but it is expensive and hard to bend into a tight coil. Loose ends will unravel and stray into the bullet's flight path.

A flat baffle will go in next, sitting on top of the roll of mesh. The hole in the center of the baffle should be 1/4 inch or a trifle more. The OD of the baffle should be .002 or .003 inch smaller than the ID of the tube. Some use fender washers for baffles, but a washer of the right size may be hard to find. A short section of the piece cut off from the barrel can be machined in the lathe. Since only one baffle is involved, it might be best to machine this component. The baffle is about 1/4 inch long, with a raised step machined into its center. Do not neglect to drill out the hole in the center. Some use 1/4 inch, but I like to go up to the next size. The step should oppose the direction of gas flow from the barrel.

There are two more components that will go into the tube at this point: another roll of mesh and the silencer's end cap. I will discuss the end cap next because its length will have a direct bearing on the length of the last roll of mesh.

The end cap will also be made from the stub left over from cutting the barrel. It will be turned to the appropriate size and drilled out to about 3/8 inch in diameter. Its length should be about 1/2 inch. It can be pressed and glued into place, TIG welded, or soft soldered. Maxim's silencers of 1910 crimped the components together in a soft iron tube. If a crimp is used, an annular (ring-shaped) groove should be cut about 1/16 inch deep around the center of the shank. A tubing or pipe cutter with a dull wheel can be used to make the crimp around the outside of the tube. Don't go too deep. Add a drop of Red Loctite to enhance the bond.

After the end cap is completed, measure for the width of the second piece of mesh. Cut the width of the mesh at least 1/8 inch shorter than you think is necessary: the second coil should not prevent full seating of the front end cap. Insert the coil of mesh and then insert and fix the front end cap into position.

Look down the tube and the rifled bore. Try to make sure that the baffle aligns with the center of the bore. If bullets hit or glance off the baffle or end cap, the unit will not be accurate. Spin the barrel in the lathe and look down the bore of the silencer. A little misalignment is permissible, but too much will allow bullet contact and promote tumbling. A small round file may be used to open up the hole in a baffle or end cap on one side to correct an alignment problem. Limit the stroke of the file so that it never contacts the delicate muzzle crown.

Put the barrel in the 10/22's action and test-fire with subsonic ammunition. The first few shots may be louder than the rest. Remove the barrel/silencer from the action. As a maker in the United States, you must have your name, city, and state engraved into the tube of the silencer, along with the model and serial number. The letters should be at least 3/32 inch tall and .010 inch deep in the tube. An engraver or jeweler should have the equipment to do the job for you. Don't use metal stamps because they will deform the tube.

Wire brush and sand the unit while it is spinning in the lathe. Finish with Oxpho-Blue or Black Matte Baking Lacquer from Brownells. If baking lacquer is used, suspend the unit in an oven with a wire or steel rod and bake at 350°F for 20 minutes.

Do not use hot bluing for the silencer. Neither the soldered joints nor the mesh will take the elevated temperature of the hot corrosive salts, and you will end up with a ruined, useless mess.

Reassemble the barrel to the action. If you used an inexpensive factory stock, you'll have to cut off the end for the barrel band and widen and deepen the barrel channel. If you used a 10/22T, the aftermarket barrel will fit in the stock perfectly. Sight the scope in and the job is done.

The silencer can be cleaned after every 1,000 rounds by dipping it in paint thinner or solvent held in a narrow plastic bottle. Dip and drain several times and then blow the system out with compressed air introduced from the breech. Always store the rifle by hanging it with the muzzle pointing straight down and the action locked open.

The silencer just described works quite well with standard-velocity or subsonic ammunition. The dominant sounds of shooting become a pressure dump out of the cycling breech and bolt noise. Few within 50 yards will notice the weapon's being fired unless they hear bullets striking or ricocheting. The silencer should never wear out as long as it is cleaned occasionally and allowed to stay dry. Although the original barrel may be replaced at any time, few who use the 10/22 in a silenced mode will want to go back to the other way.

IMPROVING YOUR RIFLE-HANDLING ABILITY

9

SHOOTING BETWEEN HEARTBEATS

The 10/22 is a fairly light rifle, and you can see your heartbeat rhythmically deflecting the crosshairs in a powerful scope as the circulatory system pulsates between roughly 2 and 4 pounds per square inch. Police snipers and benchresters are trained to shoot between heartbeats to help mitigate this effect. Every part of the body expands and contracts with every breath of air and each major heartbeat. We don't normally pay much attention to this phenomenon, but it has a considerable effect on accuracy with a rifle.

The ability to shoot between heartbeats is achieved by causing the trigger to break just as the movement from heart pulsation reaches the bottom of its cycle and before the next rise occurs. With a little practice this is easily achieved when shooting from a rest. Obviously, the window of opportunity is longer when the pulse runs 40 beats per minute, as opposed to 80 or even 160 beats per minute.

Food, mental stress, and physical activity all have a bearing on both breathing rate and pulse. It is easy to hold your breath (take a deep breath, let a little out, and then hold the rest) during a shot. It is more difficult to control your heart rate. Heart rate will be lowest during the early morning, before food is consumed. Water seems to have little effect. The ingestion of even simple food, such as a banana, will cause an increase of at least 10 beats per minute. Coffee or a sugary, caffeinated, carbonated drink will often cause an increase of as much as 50 beats per minute. Not only does the body respond to carbon dioxide, but sugar and caffeine bear almost equal responsibility. Tobacco, the extensive use of sugar and salt, stimulants, alcoholic drinks, and refined white flour have a cumulative corrosive effect on blood vessels, causing them to become stiff. This forces the heart to pump faster to deliver sufficient oxygen.

People in their 60s can have a resting heart rate in the lower 40s if they are in good physical condition as a result of diet, exercise, and the absence of stress. I am close to 60 and have a resting heart rate of about 44 beats per minute. If I cleaned up my diet, exercised more, and lost about 15 pounds, my resting heart rate would drop to as low as 40. A 20-year-old male with a perfect diet and in prime aerobic physical condition could have a resting heart rate in the low to mid-30s. When you combine quick reflexes with the superb eyesight of the young, and then add an almost two-second window of opportunity for each shot, it is obvious why many young people find it easy to do exceptionally accurate work with a rifle. With practice it is possible to override oxygen demands and mentally slow the heart rate to some degree.

For those who enjoy taking pills, a good daily multivitamin combined with extra amounts of vitamins C (6 to 8 grams per day), A, B, and D, and at least 2,000 international units of E may help to improve eyesight and mental clarity to the point where shooting scores will increase notably. Of course, as mentioned, proper nutrition, rest, and exercise are also part of the equation.

BIPODS

In situations where shots will be taken at a distance or a very high level of field accuracy is desired, a bipod is useful. I have been told that sandbags make a rifle marginally more accurate than a bipod, but I have not seen this demonstrated to my satisfaction. The difference is said to be 1/8-inch groups with sandbags as opposed to 1/4-inch groups with a bipod, but I have not seen it. As mentioned earlier, my reworked, suppressed .308 varmint rifle delivers 1/8-inch, 3-shot groups off a bipod at 100 yards. I have a hard time believing that sandbags will decrease the size of those groups. I watched two friends shooting a heavy, single-shot Johnson .50-caliber BMG rifle with a McBros action at 1,030 yards. They used a Johnson bipod set into soft tundra and had no trouble keeping their rounds inside a 4-inch circle at that great distance.

SANDBAGS

Proper use of sandbags reduces pulsation to a large extent. The rifle's forearm rests on the forward sandbag, while the butt of the rifle rests on a rear bag. The rear bag contains two projections or sand-filled "ears," which cradle the rear of the stock. The thumb and fingers of the left hand squeeze and manipulate these ears, allowing one to adjust the rifle's aim toward the target in minuscule increments. When the crosshairs appear perfectly centered on the target (with the scope's image and the "ring of darkness" perfectly centered in your optical view), you squeeze the trigger, which trips the hammer. With practice, coaching, and education a human being and a good rifle can become a united tool of incredible precision. Many otherwise normal people spend hour after pleasurable hour at a concrete shooting bench, doing nothing more than trying to shoot ever more compact groups into paper targets.

Field shooters use one or two larger, more flexible bags (filled with Styrofoam beads or corncob tumbling media instead of sand) in a similar way. If grass and vegetation are tall enough to get in the way, an adjustable bipod will prove more versatile. Many use the bipod as a forward support, holding the butt of their rifle with a bare left hand. This provides good field accuracy. If greater field accuracy is desired a small rear beanbag filled with Styrofoam beads is used to support and cradle the rifle's butt. A padded ground cloth provides a little comfort for those who hunt varmints and often shoot from the prone position.

Sandbags are available (empty) from Brownells. The specialized shooting supply houses carry bag-holding tripods as well as front and rear bags. Traditional bags are filled with clean, dry sand from a building supply store. Do not use beach sand from an ocean shore because it contains highly corrosive salts that will attract and retain water.

Sand is heavy and not particularly elastic. Pumice, vermiculite, corncob media, and

Styrofoam beads are best when a lighter weight is desired. Each material has different properties, and you are encouraged to experiment to find the one that works best for you. Styrofoam beads are lightest and have a bit of spring or bounce to them. Pumice is somewhere in the middle with regard to weight and elasticity. Vermiculite is light and fragile and will quickly be reduced in volume. Corncob media hold their shape well and are fairly lightweight. Most materials shrink over time and all bags stretch, which means you will have to add more material with use.

Those who sew (or know someone who does) can make their own bags from an old pair of jeans.

COUNTING ROUNDS AND LOCKING THE BOLT OPEN

Get into the habit of counting the number of rounds you fire. At the end of 10 rounds, or however many you've loaded into the magazine, retract and lock the bolt open. You will soon be able to do this unconsciously. With these two important skills in hand you will never accidentally "run dry" (attempt to fire a shot that goes *click* instead of *bang*), and you will have greatly reduced the possibility of an accidental or negligent discharge. Always lock the bolt open when storing or transporting the 10/22 rifle.

A WARNING ABOUT EXPLOSIVE BULLETS

Explosive bullets (with a small explosive charge in the projectile's tip) are occasionally available in .22 LR at gun shows or in firearms catalogs. Although they usually feed and fire properly and without incident, you're better off not using them in a self-loading weapon such as the 10/22. It occasionally happens that the projectile tip strikes the rear face of the barrel and explodes during the chambering process. The main propellant charge is not normally ignited, but the charge in the bullet's tip sends pieces of lead flying out the ejection port. It is for this reason that I caution against the use of exploding or explosive bullets in the 10/22 carbine.

A PROPER BACKSTOP

As the world population increases, fewer places exist where firearms can be discharged safely. Over the years I've observed quite a number of shooters firing indiscriminately "into the woods," heedless of the fact that small children might be playing out of sight in those woods or beyond. When questioned about this, a frequent response is, "Well, they shouldn't be there," or "They have no business being there." If the possible serious injury or death of a fellow human being has no impact, these careless shooters might think about the possibility of a crippling, multimillion dollar lawsuit and the consequential burden *that* would impose over the shooter's lifetime.

Typically, a proper backstop involves the edge of a hill, a soft sandbank, or a pit that one shoots into. Hard surfaces, gravel, or water will encourage a certain percentage of ricochets, and although these are not as dangerous as a direct hit, they are dangerous nonetheless. I have watched machine gun fire at a fairly generous berm at night with tracers. It is truly amazing how many of those projectiles manage to glance off and fly over the backstop. Some people shoot into open pastures or large circular bales of hay. If livestock ingest one or a number of lead bullets they run the risk of lead poisoning and possible death. If the bullets stay in the stomach they will constantly dissolve in the acid environment, sending the deadly lead out into the bloodstream. Some people use trees, which may be living or dead, as backstops. Soft woods absorb bullets fairly well when struck perpendicularly, but hardwoods are likely to cause ricochets.

A commercial bullet trap is probably the safest backstop, providing that it is large enough to catch all the bullets hurled at it. Bullet traps used to be fairly expensive, but now you can buy a good trap with a 24 x 24-inch opening for less than the wholesale cost of the basic model of the 10/22 rifle. If you are going to be shooting indoors or if you have no other reasonable backstop available, I recommend the steel bullet

Off-hand shooting should be practiced the most because it is the most difficult position to master. Photo by Mark White

The sitting position is called for when the need for accuracy is greater than what is available in the standing position. Use the long bones in your legs and arms as triangles to increase rigidity. Photo by Al Paulson

Proper form with a bipod calls for using the weak hand on the weapon's butt to position and "steer" the rifle. A four-inch diameter beanbag full of crushed walnut shell tumbling media is often used to hold the weapon's butt even steadier. Photo by Al Paulson

None of the items shown cost or weigh very much, yet each of them can become invaluable if a stoppage occurs. Photo by Mark White

trap as one of the safest options. The snail trap, in which bullets are led into a circular chamber where they spin in a circular motion until they run out of energy, is the quietest. The most expensive traps are lubricated with circulating water or oil, and the liquid traps and holds the smallest of lead particles.

For convenience, it is useful to fasten some sort of ledge or clip along the top of the trap to hold paper or cardboard targets in place. If the backstop plate rings when struck, and if this is objectionable, use contact cement to affix 2-inch-thick foam rubber to the backside. This will deaden the sound to some degree. When a normal rifle is used the sound of discharge overshadows all else; when a suppressed rifle is used the sound of the bullet striking the metal backstop is dominant and rather offensive in the absence of a loud gunshot.

One of my shooting areas is in front of a large bank of sandstone and clay. Because I do a lot of shooting, and because I am concerned about ricochets, I mounted a 3 x 3-foot plate of 1/4-inch-thick steel at a 45-degree angle to the ground. Since I am also interested in keeping the sound level down, I piled dirt on top of the back side of the plate to deaden the sound of projectile impact. Those bullets that strike the plate are deflected downward into the earth. It is a simple system, easy to set up, effective, and quiet. The simple angled plate provides considerable peace of mind. If I ever want to reclaim the lead to cast into bullets, the spent .22 LR projectiles remain fairly well concentrated in one area.

A FIELD KIT

Whenever I go afield or to a shooting range I carry a field kit that allows me to clear stoppages and make emergency adjustments on the spot. This kit has been assembled after some 40 years of occasionally painful experience. More items could be added, but not much should be taken away. The pieces are usually stowed or wrapped in a 12 x 12-inch mechanic's hand towel and fit in a surplus field pouch or a small sushi tin.

Screwdrivers

The first item—and the one most used—is a small screwdriver with a 2 1/4-inch shaft and a 1/8-inch-wide blade. This is most useful for tightening small scope-mounting screws and for prying stuck, spent shells out of a dirty chamber.

A second screwdriver with a somewhat larger 3/8-inch-wide blade is helpful to remove the main stock/action screw so that the barreled action can be separated from the stock if field-stripping becomes necessary. Also, if a scope adjustment is called for, the screwdriver with the 3/8-inch blade is more positive than a dime or a penny.

Leatherman Tool

I also carry a multifunction Leatherman tool. It has a variety of tips that occasionally come in handy, although the lack of symmetry makes it more difficult for turning screws.

Lubricant

If shells seem to stick, the most likely cause is a dirty chamber. A drop of oil and a quick scrub with a bent nylon bore brush will usually set things right. A small plastic vial (of the type normally used for eye drops or lens-cleaning fluid) will hold a bit of the proper lubricant. Test to make sure that the oil of choice won't dissolve the container.

Magnifying Glass

For those of us over the age of 50, a small magnifying glass or loupe is useful for observing the arrows and divisions on scope adjustments. The eye loupe is also useful for removing painful thorns and briars, which are often picked up in the field. Optical magnification is also beneficial when turning small screws and trying to figure out why some part of the 10/22's action has become nonfunctional. Occasionally, the base mount on the top of the 10/22's receiver will work loose, even though it may have been screwed and glued into position. This will result in a shifting or fading zero, and the only remedy is to remove the scope and retighten the base. The magnifying glass or eye loupe is useful when retightening the screws. (Remember: the base will have to be reglued later, or the base mount will become loose again.)

Cleaning Rod

A cleaning rod is also useful to have if a bullet gets stuck in the bore or some other bore obstruction exists. I prefer a solid rod for this, but if a sectional rod is all you have, that will have to do. Driving the obstruction out from the muzzle is most expedient, but you run the very serious risk of damaging the crown in doing so.

Wrenches

A special 5/32-inch Allen wrench made by Bondhus will allow the barrel to be removed so that a slug can be driven out from the rear. A regular 5/32-inch Allen wrench can also be used, but the Bondhus wrench has a sort of universal ball on the long end that greatly facilitates rapid removal of the two barrel-retention screws.

If the scope mounts are held on with Allen screws, you should also carry a wrench that fits those screws. A 6d (or 2-inch) nail or a small scribe should also be carried. It can be used to loosen small particles in the action and to remove and clean the extractor and its spring and plunger, should that be necessary.

(If the bore obstruction can't be driven out, that usually means two or more slugs are lodged into one lump in the bore. Stop at that point and take the barrel to a gun shop later for proper removal of the obstruction and inspection of the bore. The obstruction can't be "shot out" with another cartridge, so don't even bother trying. There are a lot of used 10/22 barrels around of late, and one would do well to pick one up for a spare (of course, I wouldn't carry a spare barrel in the field, but I might keep one in my pickup truck).

Illumination Tools

I also carry a small candle in a little aluminum cup, a book of waterproof matches, and a small penlight. Sometimes it is dark when a repair needs to be made.

• • •

That's about it for field corrections. Odd things like a broken hammer or broken springs don't normally happen with the 10/22. You are more likely to encounter a clogged barrel than a broken firing pin. Dirt and fouling may accumulate, but moving parts in the receiver rarely if ever fail.

AMMUNITION

10

I will begin this chapter with a brief treatise on velocity, flight characteristics, and terminal ballistics. When the priming ring on a .22 LR shell is struck (or rapidly crushed), it begins to ignite. The burning process soon spreads to the main charge of nitrated cellulose behind the bullet. Pressure rises inside the cartridge, accelerating the burn rate. If the powder charge was dumped on a plate and lit with a match, it would take between one and three seconds to burn, depending on atmospheric temperature and humidity. The accelerated burn rate inside a typical cartridge is between .1 and .4 second, depending primarily on temperature, ultimate pressure, and the type of powder involved. The greater the pressure, the greater the heat. The greater the heat, the more rapid the burn rate.

TIME DELAY

The time between trigger pull and bullet exit may seem instantaneous, but it is not. It should be noted that the loudness of the report somehow compresses the time interval in a shooter's mind. When firing a suppressed firearm I have noticed that the interval between pulling the trigger and bullet movement *seemed* considerably longer. Of course, a rifle with a faster lock time, a shorter barrel, and cartridges with quicker burn characteristics will reduce the time delay somewhat—leading to a weapon with greater inherent field accuracy. At any rate, a loud report overshadows any time delay that you may perceive.

If a rifle is not held in a rest, the trigger will be pulled in an attempt to discharge a shot as the sight's crosshairs swing by the exact center of the target. As steady as we try to make ourselves, we are always wavering to some degree as we stand upright in the field. This is also true to a lesser extent when shooting from a bench. Here we have the pulsation from our heartbeat as a major factor of movement. A set trigger (or a two-stage trigger), a lighter hammer, and a stronger hammer spring will chop 20 to 30 percent from the total time delay between the moment of the decision to fire and the precise instant of the bullet's departure. A barrel with a weight or pendulum on the end will, of course, reduce the rapidity of the swing or waver. Note that putting a weight on a barrel's muzzle will be more effective than simply using a heavy, straight-sectioned (untapered) barrel.

It is a little-known fact that .22 LR target ammunition (as opposed to generic, high-speed ammunition) is charged with a faster burning type of powder (in a slightly reduced amount) to get the bullet upset, plugged into the rifling, and moving in a shorter time. Once the charge inside the shell reaches a fairly high pressure level it begins to move the bullet out of the case.

There are three main elements that hold a bullet in its case: inertia, the crimp between case mouth and bullet, and the throat (which is the transition between the chamber and the rifling). The higher the pressure rise before bullet movement, the greater the efficiency of the powder burn. Handloaders of 9mm and .45 ACP cartridges find that they can increase a given velocity of a bullet not by increasing the powder charge but simply by crimping their bullets into the cases with more force. Those who tightly crimp their bullets can expect about 100 fps more velocity. Those who both crimp and glue their bullets in place can get an increase of as much as 200 fps.

Most 10/22 chamberings have a section of freebore, which allows a bullet to exit a case before it encounters the greater friction of the throat and the rifling. Most aftermarket 10/22 target barrels use a Bentz style of chamber, which allows the bullet to encounter the rifling at the same time it is trying to overcome inertia and pull itself free from the case mouth crimp. When all three factors work in unison, the net result is a higher chamber pressure and a more efficient powder burn.

It should be reiterated that most of the burning in a typical .22 LR takes place before the bullet exits its case. After that, rapid expansion and cooling from contact with the bore greatly reduce the remaining ability of the charge to burn. The powder charge lacks sufficient oxygen to burn completely. This is evidenced by reignition at both the muzzle and the breech as the mass of gas and partially burned powder is exposed to the air, which roughly is one-fifth oxygen. Experiments have been conducted in which a cartridge is filled with pure oxygen and gunpowder. This boosts efficiency. But since there is no way to hold the oxygen in place over time, the practice is not in use at present. In the loose chamber of a 10/22 rifle barrel, a typical .22 LR bullet achieves 62 to 65 percent of its velocity in the first inch or two of acceleration.

It is generally acknowledged that the violent destructive force of a high-speed bullet does not occur until the projectile reaches a velocity of 2,200 fps. The fastest .22 LR cartridge currently on the planet is CCI's Stinger, which uses more than 3 grains of powder behind a 30-grain, hollowpoint projectile. In a 16-inch barrel with a tight chamber, the Stinger will reach a velocity approaching 1,600 fps, which is well below the critical 2,200-fps threshold. The tissue destruction caused by all .22 LR rounds is therefore of the first order, and it would seem reasonable to assume that velocities beyond 1,100 fps are not gifted with the supernatural powers associated with very fast varmint rifles. Therefore, as long as foot-pounds of energy remain similar and as long as the construction of a bullet is optimal for its planned use, you are best served by a bullet that travels *below* the speed of sound. We will get to the reason for this very shortly.

THE SONIC PHENOMENON

Once a bullet leaves its barrel, the initial velocity will have considerable bearing on inherent accuracy. While increased velocity is generally considered to be a good thing, the most prominent obstacle to accuracy is the sonic barrier. At sea level, in dry, 65°F air, the speed of sound is generally recognized to be 1,089 fps, commonly referred to as Mach 1.

On 14 October 1947, U.S. Air Force Capt. Chuck Yeager became the first person to pilot an aircraft, the Bell X-1, faster than the speed of sound. For aircraft, the sound barrier was extremely difficult to break because of the considerable buffeting and instability that occur at this critical velocity. At Mach .97 Captain Yeager had a serious battle on his hands just keeping the aircraft pointed in a straight direction. Once he was well beyond Mach 1.2, flight returned to normal. However, when he dropped back into the critical range on the way back down, the instability returned, and the battle for control resumed until the speed of his X-1 dropped below the velocity of sound.

The same thing occurs with any bullet that hovers in this critical transonic range. Bullets that greatly exceed the speed of sound are quite accurate, as long as their velocity decay does not bring them into the transonic range before impact. The standard .308 military round is a good example. It is very accurate up to 600 yards. At that point it begins to waver a bit, but it will retain fair accuracy up until about 800 yards. At roughly 850 yards its velocity usually drops solidly into the transonic range, which is from 1,040 to 1,282 fps, or 300 to 400 meters per second. At that speed, the relatively long, pointy, boattailed .308 bullet will become so unstable that it will often tumble end over end, quickly shedding velocity and accuracy in the process.

We've said all this to say that when a .22 LR bullet is launched at roughly 1,350 fps (typical high-speed .22 velocity), the chances are very good that its velocity will decay into the unstable transonic range before it reaches its target, seriously affecting accuracy. The soft .22 bullet lacks the hardness to retain a sharp point, so most tend to have round noses, which helps to keep them more stable.

A short, round-nosed bullet tends to be very stable. It will track well when penetrating most any medium. The result is that most high-speed .22 LR bullets will not tumble in the transonic

range, but they will lose stability and accuracy. Very fast (more than 1,400 fps) .22 LR bullets made of common soft lead will often melt at the base and strip at the lands, coating the bore with lead in the process. This is, of course, detrimental to accuracy. The most accurate .22 LR bullets will have a muzzle velocity of approximately 1,000 fps. It is possible to get extreme accuracy with velocities up to 1,050, but the odds favor the slightly slower speeds.

MATCHING AMMUNITION

With regard to ammunition, you can select the most appropriate brand and lot of .22 LR ammunition for your particular firearm based on a number of factors.

If cost is the only consideration it is a simple matter to check prices and go with what is least expensive. Often, discount stores such as Costco, Sam's, or Wal-Mart will advertise and sell promotional ammunition at bargain prices. Distributors and stocking dealers will also advertise special deals made available to them by CCI, Federal, Remington, Winchester, or other manufacturers. Buy a little and try it. If it works well, go back and buy a lot.

Many suppressed 10/22 shooters are interested in very high levels of silence. Since inexpensive target ammunition is subsonic, it is normally fairly quiet. A chronograph is useful in checking velocities at various temperatures. By the way, chronographs are usually accurate within 30 fps. One day we tested two chronographs of the same model and brand against each other by shooting rounds over both of them at the same time. Rarely did they agree with each other. Sometimes they were within 2 fps. Sometimes the first one would read 20 fps faster; another time the second one read 20 fps faster.

If testing ammunition from a particular rifle on a cool day, remember that it is almost guaranteed to shoot faster on a hot day. Again, my preferred velocity for subsonic ammunition is 1,000 fps. Interestingly, U.S. personnel involved in covert operations during World War II

THE ULTIMATE RUGER 10/22 MANUAL AND USER'S GUIDE

specified that ammunition for suppressed weapons have a velocity of 1,000 fps. It is nice to know that the laws of physics (unlike gun laws) haven't changed in 60 years.

If extreme accuracy is a concern, the proper match of .22 LR ammunition to your particular rifle is an important link in the equation. Usually a shooter will buy just one box of a number of different lots and brands of .22 ammo. Some stocking dealers will occasionally offer a deal on "sampler" assortments of ammunition to help their customers find the best for their particular firearm. Most of those enthusiasts I know will try a sampling of 20 or more variations at one sitting.

The sampling exercise is often conducted as follows. Each box in the assortment is labeled with a number (e.g., 1 through 20). A series of targets is likewise numbered with a felt-tip marker. Some shooters use small targets in clusters of five. Others use 16 x 24-inch sheets of white poster board with square, black target pasters placed and numbered at selected intervals. The target is stapled to a stand 50 yards away from a sturdy benchrest. Five shots of each variation are carefully discharged at each numbered target. Here is where experience and skill on a benchrest will prove valuable.

After the targets are shot, retrieve them for examination. Many groupings will be excessively large, so exclude their corresponding lot numbers immediately. Usually, four or five groups will be notably smaller than the others. Fire a second set of five shots of each of these to determine which variations hold the most promise. The second round of targets is often an affirmation of the first. More lots of ammunition are then purchased, with cost, accuracy, and availability being determining factors. Never expect that a different lot of ammunition purchased a year or two later will have the same characteristics— sometimes they do, but they usually don't. There are times when dedicated shooters may spend from 20 to 50 cents a round for an important match. In the real world, however, your testing should reveal a brand and lot that will be suitable for 2 to 3 cents a round.

A WARNING ABOUT EXPLODING BULLETS

Exploding bullets, with a small explosive charge in the projectile's tip, are occasionally available in .22 LR at gun shows or in catalogs. Although they usually feed and fire properly, you would be better off not using them in a self-loading weapon, such as the 10/22. It has occasionally happened that such a projectile tip strikes the rear face of the barrel and explodes during the chambering process. The main propellant charge is not normally ignited, but the charge in the bullet's tip can send pieces of lead flying out the ejection port. Again, I caution against the use of exploding bullets in the 10/22 carbine. However, if this warning is ignored, safety goggles are highly recommended.

THE PERFORMANCE OF BULLETS ON SMALL GAME

When it comes to hunting, many people instinctively reach for a box of high-speed hollowpoints. The hollowpoint .22 is an interesting concept that only works in a very narrow set of conditions. On larger animals the cavity plugs up with hair and refuses to open. At other times the shock of impact will cause the tip to open up rapidly, but the soft lead lacks integrity and the opened tip separates from the rest of the bullet, leaving a small lead base that doesn't have enough momentum to penetrate. This causes a lot of superficial damage but won't kill humanely. The soft hollowpoints do work fairly well on very small game but often fail on animals weighing more than 6 pounds.

The U.S. Army's Martin L. Fackler, M.D., FACS, did extensive research on wound ballistics. Some of that research revealed the fact that the permanent wound cavity (as opposed to the temporary wound cavity, which occurs in elastic tissue) is often the most important. Aside from inelastic brain and liver tissue, the remainder of a small animal's body consists of elastic tissue (muscle, blood vessels, and skin), which temporarily expands with the passing of a bullet and then

Aguila SE is a round of standard weight that will be subsonic in most weapons. It won't always cycle in many 10/22 actions. Lapua's 48-grain Scoremax is expensive, subsonic, accurate, and very quiet, especially in a suppressed weapon. It also cycles very well in most rifles. Aguila SSS carries a 60-grain projectile, currently the heaviest in the industry. It has a modest velocity of from 650 to 800 fps in most 10/22 rifles. Cycling is problematic in two ways: (1) the short shell pops out before pressure drops enough, resulting in propellant gas and particulates blasting out of the action and into the shooter's face; and (2) the short shell lacks the mass or a normal .22 LR shell and thus often stays in the action, preventing the next round from cycling. It is a rare 10/22 rifle that will cycle SSS without problems. Accuracy of the SSS round is typically poor to fair.

contracts to its original conformation. The death of a small animal is caused primarily by the round's severing a vital nerve or penetrating a vital organ. Blood is lost through the permanent wound channel, which is essentially the diameter of the flat point of the bullet that passed through the area.

CCI used this information to develop what it calls the Small-Game Bullet (SGB). This bullet has a slightly flattened tip and is made of a hardened lead alloy, which holds its shape well. It performs very effectively on small game of 6 to 30 pounds. Expect about 1,170 fps with the SGB out of a 10/22 factory barrel and about 1,210 fps from an aftermarket target barrel. Accuracy with the SGB is usually excellent, but the only way to tell is by firing them through your 10/22 at a paper target from a rest. Some competitors I know use the SGB in BR50 matches—they are that good.

CCI's Stinger is often used for hunting. It contains a 30-grain bullet, which usually moves out at a brisk 1,600 fps. Stingers are usually not accurate, but the only way to tell for sure is to fire them through your rifle.

SUPPRESSORS AND 10/22 ANIMAL CONTROL

11

A number of law enforcement and professional personnel employ a suppressed 10/22 in the line of duty. Police officers on drug raids often use a silenced .22 rifle to take out yard lights or tires on potential escape vehicles prior to an assault. Ranchers, farmers, timber growers, gamekeepers, park rangers, golf course maintenance personnel, groundskeepers, and animal control officers all need to use a quiet rifle with moderate power to eliminate pests, predators, and injured or diseased animals. Where the ultimate in silence and a low profile is called for, I feel that a suppressed .22 single-shot or bolt-action rifle is most effective. Those in the profession, however, continue to use the semiautomatic 10/22 because it provides rapid and multiple follow-up shots, should they be necessary.

Suppressors (silencers) for this carbine come in three different forms: muzzle can, integral, and hybrid. The muzzle can is a relatively small device, which is screwed or clamped to a barrel's muzzle. The muzzle can is the easiest to build or install. Power and accuracy of the firearm are normally not degraded by the can, but subsonic ammunition should be used to keep the sound level as low as possible. Although the muzzle report will be greatly diminished, any projectile traveling beyond 1,100 fps will break the sound barrier, creating an awful racket in the process. It has been proven that gunfire noise is the most objectionable sound to the public at large.

During World War II British and U.S. inventors developed the integral style of silencer. This system involves expansion holes or ports drilled through the barrel, directly into the bore, and surprisingly close to the weapon's chamber. These holes vent or dump propellant gas early in the firing cycle, slowing the projectile somewhat and softening the noise of the weapon's report. Baffles and expansion chambers in the end of the integral can are then able to mask what is left of the report to an even greater degree.

An integral can is often more silent than a

muzzle can. However, the integral system usually delivers lower projectile velocity and traps more crud in the process. The pressurized primary expansion chamber also back-flushes great quantities of filth and corruption into the 10/22's action. In addition, the shortened power stroke (the bullet usually only moves about 3 inches in the typical 10/22 barrel before gas begins to be diverted) typical of an integral system robs vital energy that the rifle's action needs for effective cycling. Not only does the weapon get dirty fast, it also lacks the push required to extract and reload. This results in a rifle doomed to reliability problems.

A hybrid system uses a shorter, unported 10-inch barrel attached to a muzzle can. Hybrid systems are about as effective as muzzle cans, but they allow a cleaner powder burn and induce more of the crud to move downrange instead of into the 10/22's action. The 10-inch barrel does not significantly degrade the rifle's power level or its ability to cycle.

Both integral and hybrid systems are usually housed inside a long, 1 to 1.25-inch-diameter tube that contains both barrel and suppressor components. This tube resembles a relatively innocent bull target barrel. If the unit is machined properly the average citizen is not able to tell the difference between the two. A muzzle can has a more distinctive (some say sinister) appearance because the end of the barrel is larger. When properly executed, the accuracy potential of all three systems should be identical.

All the studies on the subject have shown that the smaller and quieter a rifle is, the less it will intimidate/threaten/annoy/anger private citizens, who are likely to try to prevent the animal control officer from doing his or her job. A firearm that is physically shorter and properly camouflaged will have a lower profile than one that is longer and shinier. A rifle that doesn't make much noise will draw less attention than an unsuppressed firearm. A low profile is important in this profession. One must make an effort to remain out of the public eye by shooting from concealment whenever possible, capturing and

retaining spent cartridges, and properly disposing of animal carcasses.

The ideal animal control bullet should be heavy and of soft lead and travel at around 1,000 fps. Ammunition that moves somewhat faster runs the risk of producing a ballistic crack under certain atmospheric conditions. Most .22 target ammunition is designed to move at a modest subsonic velocity and has a bullet weight of about 40 grains.

The U.S. market is strong enough that both Remington and Winchester manufacture subsonic hollowpoint ammunition for suppressed animal control. Lapua manufactures an accurate, subsonic (about 1,020 fps) round with a heavier, 48-grain projectile. Aguila manufactures accurate subsonic rounds in both 40 and 60 grains. Most subsonic .22 LR ammunition is inherently more accurate than supersonic ammunition because it is more stable in flight, with the possible exception of Aguila's 60-grain projectile, which is so long that it may not stabilize in most 10/22 barrels. The round in question requires a barrel with a twist approaching a full turn in 10 inches or a specially porter barrel. Engel Ballistic Research is experimenting with a .22 LR round approaching 65 grains, and this is said to be stable in a standard 10/22 barrel.

Typically, squirrels, chucks, rats, pigeons, crows, and magpies are shot in the chest. Rabbits may be shot in either the head or the chest, at ranges of up to 100 yards. Coyotes and feral dogs should be shot in the lower rear portion of the brain if at all possible. Animals over 20 pounds are more reliably disposed of with a more powerful cartridge than the .22 LR, but you must use what you have when the opportunity avails. Feral cats should be shot in the chest because head shots are often not reliable for some reason. Poisonous snakes should be struck in the rear portion of the head whenever possible. Usually the first shot is all you get at a predator, so you must learn to be fast and accurate in shooting. Because many shots will penetrate entirely, you must be sure of a proper backstop. This is especially important when exercising animal control around an airport or a park. This last point cannot be overemphasized.

Long shots are often quite effective if they are well directed. I once saw a very large seagull taken at 400 measured yards near an airport runway with a single shot from a suppressed 10/22. The contractor had to dispose of hundreds of gulls each month, so he was quite practiced in the art of long-distance delivery. A medium jet had crashed with considerable loss of life because of multiple bird strikes, so the pressure was on to eliminate any bird that showed a predisposition to flight near the runways.

A folding bipod, a crisp 3-pound trigger, and a good 6x scope are valuable aids to accuracy. A range of 80 to 100 yards is within reason for a good marksman. In some situations the suppressed system will be so effective that it will allow as many as six birds to be taken in a row before the survivors take flight. Some shots on rats and cats will be taken at 30 feet in basements and crawl spaces. Carcasses are best handled with gloves and tongs and transferred to opaque plastic bags for disposal as soon as possible. In larger operations a shooter and a bagger make an effective team.

The best opportunities for shots are usually near dusk and dawn. Bait is often useful for wary varmints. One should use a golf cart or small pickup truck to mask and cover the retrieval of an animal if public relations is a problem, as it usually is near an airport. Municipalities, airports (especially those near coastlines), water control boards, parks, and service districts will often contract animal control on a part-time basis when they do not have dedicated personnel to handle a specific problem. Airports, parks, and golf courses call for a low-profile approach of the highest order.

Some argue that the mild .22 CB Long cartridge is absolutely silent when fired in an unsuppressed rifle. That is patently untrue. Most sound instrument readings measure 131 dB for this gunfire signature. The same report from a 10/22 rifle fitted with a muzzle can will measure about 109 decibels (dB). A standard-velocity .22 LR round will measure about 138 dB,

unsuppressed, and 111 to 113 dB suppressed. Since the decibel scale progresses geometrically, a decrease of from 30 to 40 dB represents an order of magnitude from 900 to 1,600. An average suppressor can reduce the sound signature to a mere 1/1,000 of what it normally would have been. On a day with average outdoor background noise, everyone within 200 yards will notice the gunfire noise from either round. This is especially so if more than one round is fired. Suppressed, the gunfire will be noticed by few people within 40 yards. Those who do hear the sound will not register the event as a rifle shot, and that is the important thing. The sound of a subsonic bullet slipping through the air will be a barely audible whizzing sound, certainly less than that of an arrow from a bow. Since the action noise of the 10/22 is substantial, that clacking noise will be the dominant sound.

Many muzzle cans are detachable, but some for a 10/22 rifle are permanently mounted to the barrel. A rifle used for animal control should be reliably accurate. A permanently mounted muzzle can tends to dampen barrel vibrations; thus the barrel will cause its bullets to stay solidly on target. Many screw-on cans will walk bullets around a target face if the threads loosen. The simple act of removing and replacing some screw-on muzzle cans may result in a substantial change in scope zero. A single-point, screw-on mount can be quite fragile. Something that is easily bent or broken does not belong on a rifle used for this type of work. The hybrid system offers great strength combined with a relatively innocent, compact look. My company, Sound Technology, developed a 1 3/8 x 8-inch muzzle can with left-hand threads especially for a heavy-barreled 10/22. We have been pleased with the repeatable accuracy this system has demonstrated.

It is possible to use a two-point mount to attach a screw-on muzzle can. Such a mount usually has a threaded portion at the muzzle and a tapered seat about 4 or 5 inches behind the muzzle. The two-point mount is stable, quite strong, and fairly reliable. If executed properly it does allow removal and replacement without a

This weapon fits easily in a small knapsack. If ammunition is properly tailored to the right species, no weapon other than a 10/22 is needed for animal control. Photo by Al Paulson

loss of zero. It is possible to temporarily fuse a single-point mount in place with Red Loctite or soft solder, but the system will not be as strong as a hybrid suppressor or one fastened with a two-point mount.

In summary, when people ask, I always recommend the inexpensive muzzle can as the first choice for suppressing the 10/22 carbine. The simple can is trouble free and does not alter the reliability of the action. If a lower profile is required I then recommend a short, 10-inch, heavy barrel inside a suppressed hybrid system. A 10-inch barrel is more accurate than a factory 18 1/2-inch barrel and will deliver 97 percent of the velocity. If the short barrel is permanently fused (welded) to a 16-inch steel tube, the weapon does not have to be registered as a short-barreled rifle. Of course, if the weapon is to be owned by a municipality or a police department there will be no registration fees required and the system may be of any convenient length. I would never recommend an integrally suppressed system for a 10/22 (although I make and sell quite a few of them) because there is simply no point in having a complex, high-maintenance, highly efficient suppressor quieter than the rifle's action noise.

If a person wants extreme suppression, I try to steer him toward a bolt-action rifle. As a practical matter, the use of subsonic ammunition in a typical suppressed system will mask the event to the point where no one will notice it.

The clack of the 10/22's bolt hitting the 1/4-inch-diameter steel bolt-stop pin will be the dominant noise, and that is the sound that will carry farthest. Again, I have on occasion replaced the steel bolt-stop pin with one made of nylon. That reduced the rearward bolt noise somewhat. I have seen a piece of Neoprene rubber fuel hose slipped over the 1/4-inch bolt-stop pin, but that requires removing metal in the receiver and enlarging the groove in the rear of the 10/22's bolt.

An old trick that military folks used on covert ops was to wire or tape a small cloth bag over the rifle or machine gun's ejection port. This performed double duty by silencing the bolt noise somewhat and capturing spent cases. I've seen these used on the 10/22. The bags were inflated with propellant gas, the sound level decreased, and the empty cases were captured perfectly. If a jam occurs it is important to be able to strip the bag off quickly so the stoppage can be cleared.

Suppressors are legal to own privately in the following states: Alaska, Alabama, Arkansas, Arizona, Colorado, Connecticut, Florida, Georgia, Idaho, Indiana, Kentucky, Louisiana, Maine, Maryland, Montana, North Dakota, North Carolina, New Mexico, New Hampshire, Nevada, Ohio, Oklahoma, Oregon, Pennsylvania, South Carolina, South Dakota, Tennessee, Texas, Utah, Virginia, Washington, Wisconsin, West Virginia, and Wyoming. They may be owned by Class 3 dealers and Class 2 manufacturers in California, Iowa, Kansas, Massachusetts, and Missouri. Almost any government agency, municipality, or police department may own a silencer in any state.

SUPPLIERS

Aircraft Spruce and Specialty Co.
Western Branch:
    225 Airport Circle, Corona, CA 91720
Eastern Branch:
    900 S. Pine Hill Rd., Griffin, GA 30223

This is a supplier of aircraft parts, primarily aluminum and 4130 steel aircraft tubing. Its catalog is $6.

Boyds'
25376 403rd Ave.
Mitchell, SD 57301
www.boyds.com

Boyds' has purchased the material and tooling from the major wooden stock makers in this country and is currently producing the most popular lines of wooden stocks, including those for the 10/22 rifle.

Brownells
200 S. Front St.
Montezuma, IA 50171

Brownells is a supplier for gunsmiths. Sales are usually restricted to federal firearms license holders. Brownells has a huge catalog with more than 26,000 items—many unavailable from any other source—and almost everything is in stock. Quality is normally good, but prices are a bit high. This is a good source for chambering reamers, crowning tools, stocks, barrels, mounting bases, scope rings, scopes, and iron sights. Brownells also has technical support staff who will talk to you (on your nickel) about firearm modifications and repair.

Bushnell Sports Optics
9200 Cody
Overland Park, KS 66214

Bushnell Sports Optics provides scopes, binoculars, and laser range finders. Its first finder, the Lite Speed 400, revolutionized distance hunting. It used an accurately directed beam of light to bounce off a target, and an accurate timer to measure the time for the beam's trip out and back. Its Yardage Pro 400, 600, and 800 series is easy to use and very, very accurate. A number of people hunt varmints with 10/22 target rifles—at ranges up to 400 yards. They carry a range scale taped to their stock and a range finder to "lase" the target with the invisible light beam. With practice, it is possible to find the range (accurate to a yard or meter), dial the appropriate adjustment on the scope, and get a first-round hit. Reflective surfaces (e.g., trees, rocks, traffic signs) are usually more "lasable" than furry targets. Silencers are often used to allow more shots to be discharged before the varmints become wary. The Bushnell Yardage Pro range finder has changed the way many people hunt. A subsonic round loses very little velocity at extreme range. Given that there is little wind, long-distance shooting becomes a problem of elevation and steadiness. The affordable range finder has been a tremendous advantage to long-distance varmint hunters. Street prices usually range from $180 to $320, with the least expensive model weighing about a pound and the most expensive model about 12 ounces. Bushnell does not normally sell directly to the consumer.

Butler Creek
290 Arden Dr.
Belgrade, MT 59714

Butler Creek makes polymer stocks in the full and folding configurations, heavy and light aftermarket barrels, a target stock with a clever built-in bipod, scope covers, sling swivels, slings, and straps. Its designers have a good eye for line and form. Butler Creek stocks add to the accuracy potential of the 10/22 rifle and are light, durable, and quite handsome. The U.S. government has discouraged folding stocks in recent years, so the day may come when the source has dried up entirely. Used 10/22 rifles with folding stocks are occasionally available on the private market. Butler Creek also made 20- and 30-round magazines for the 10/22 until the 1994 ban. These are still available to a limited degree. Those with steel feed lips are the most desirable; those with plastic feed lips wear quickly. Because the 10/22 barrel lacks a feed ramp, the action is prone to malfunction in feeding. A good magazine is critical in this regard. Butler Creek magazines are only fair with regard to feeding malfunctions, but they constitute the best of the high-capacity magazines. A wide variety of distributors and dealers sell Butler Creek Products.

Cabela's
812 13th Ave.
Sidney, NE 69160

Cabela's is a catalog retailer of various outdoor and shooting-related products. Prices are fair, and delivery is usually rapid. The catalog will alert the reader to new products as they become available in the marketplace.

Centurion Ordnance
13750 US 281 N. St. E.
San Antonio, TX 78232

Centurion is the importer for the Mexican ammunition company Aguila. Aguila produces a wide variety of innovative ammunition, including .22 rimfire ammunition. Of note is the .22 Colibri, a 20-grain pellet that is propelled with priming material only, at a velocity of roughly 400 fps. This must be cycled by hand in the 10/22 but is in demand by animal control personnel for use in collecting pigeons from barns, warehouses, and aircraft hangers. This round makes very little noise when discharged from an unsuppressed weapon and will normally not penetrate roofing metal or break windows. Another round worthy of note is the .22 SSS or Sniper SubSonic, a 60-grain projectile that travels at roughly 800 fps (instead of the advertised 950 fps) from a standard 10/22 barrel. Unfortunately, for suppressed work in the 10/22, the short case ejects too early in the firing cycle, resulting in a loud "pop" from the ejection port, which is hard on the shooter's hearing. The round exhibits a considerable drop in trajectory yet has excellent penetration, which may be useful in some applications. Also available is the .22 Super Maximum, a light projectile that travels at an advertised 1,750 fps. Like CCI's Stinger, the Super Maximum is normally not very accurate, but it is interesting to shoot.

Choate Machine and Tool
116 Lovers Lane
Bald Knob, AR 72010

Choate is the acknowledged king of plastic accessories for the firearms industry. It produces hundreds of innovative items that are sturdy, utilitarian, and well made. Sales are usually made through distributors and dealers.

Clark Custom Guns
3336 Shootout Lane
Princeton, LA 71067
www.clarkcustomguns.com

Clark performs expensive custom modifications to 10/22 actions, triggers, etc. It also sells barrels and stocks from other manufacturers. Clark's prices are high, but the work and quality are both excellent. Its barrels are much harder than most, are usually very accurate, and tend to last a long time.

Clymer Manufacturing Co.
1645 West Hamlin Rd.
Rochester Hills, MI 48309

Clymer makes chambering reamers, crowning tools, scope ring reamers, etc.

Custom Quality Products
345 West Girard St.
Madison Heights, MI 48071

This outfit makes solid and see-through scope mounts, Weaver-style bases, and quick-detachable scope mount rings. The material is aluminum, while the screws are high-tensile steel. Prices are affordable, and strength and quality are superb. Custom's aluminum rings may be the strongest available. Sales are usually through dealers and distributors.

Dillon Precision Products
8009 East Dillons Way
Scottsdale, AZ 85260
www.dillonprecision.com

Dillon primarily deals with reloading equipment, but it also retails a number of 10/22 accessories, such as barrels and stocks. It sells a very good line of eye protection, which you will need if shooting at steel plates. Quality and service are excellent.

Graf & Sons
4050 S. Highway 54
Mexico, MO 65265

Graf stocks Winchester and Remington ammunition and normally sells to dealers.

H-S Precision
1301 Turbine Dr.
Rapid City, SD 55703

H-S fabricates fiberglass and Kevlar/carbon fiber stocks. Its prices are very expensive, but its products are usually of quality. It will sell direct.

Harris Engineering
Barlow, KY 42024
www.cyberteklabs.com/harris/main/htm

The Harris line of bipods is the standard of the industry. These bipods are very strong for the weight and are well engineered. Sales are usually through distributors and dealers.

JGS
100 Main Sumner Rd.
Coos Bay, OR 97420

JGS manufactures chambering reamers and muzzle-crowning tools. Prices are high, and quality is good.

Leatherman Tool Group
Box 20595
Portland, OR 97294

Leatherman was the first to manufacture a multifunctional pocket tool incorporating stainless steel pliers, screwdrivers, etc. This tool is very useful in the field. Its products are sold mostly through dealers and distributors.

McMillan Fiberglass Stocks
21421 N 14th Ave.
Phoenix, AZ 85027
mfsinc@indirect.com

McMillan manufactures fiberglass and Kevlar stocks that are high quality, lightweight, stable, and very expensive.

Millett Sights
7275 Murdy Circle
Huntington Beach, CA 92647
www.millettsights.com

Millett sells good-quality sights and scope mounting systems that are normally sold through dealers and distributors.

NECO
536-C Stone Rd.
Benicia, CA 94510
www.neconos.com

NECO is a supplier of bore-lapping compounds, moly-coating supplies, accuracy gauges, and firearm lubricants.

ProEars
Box 930
Dewey, AZ 86327-0930

If you are going to shoot an unsuppressed rifle you should be using hearing protection. ProEars are expensive but good. Any ear protection is better than no protection.

Ram-Line
Box 38
Onalaska, WI 54650

Ram-Line manufactures stocks, magazines, and 10/22 accessories. In the past, these have not held up well.

Remington Arms Co.
870 Remington Dr.
Madison, NC 27025-0700

In addition to firearms, Remington also manufactures an extensive line of rimfire ammunition. Its sales are through dealers and distributors.

SacUps
1611 Jamestown Rd.
Morgantown, NC 28655

This outfit manufactures silicone-treated gun

sacks to protect various rifles and shotguns. The sacks are far too long for the 10/22 but can be cut and resewn. A sack will cover a weapon with a scope, but it is difficult getting it on and off. It is a nice concept poorly executed. Buy one only if you have an unscoped weapon to protect. Be prepared to cut it off and resew the end. Prices are very reasonable, and sales are through distributors and dealers.

Sound Technology
Box 391
Pelham, AL 35124
www.hypercon.com/soundtech

Sound Technology is a manufacturer of silencers for firearms.

Stoney Point Products
1219 N. Front St.
New Ulm, MN 56073-0234
www.stoneypoint.com

This firm sells telescoping bipods and monopods to aid in steadying a rifle when firing.

Sturm, Ruger & Co.
200 Ruger Rd.
Prescott, AZ 86301
www.ruger-firearms.com

Tasco
2889 Commerce Parkway
Miramar, FL 33025
lacplan@tascosales.com or www.tascosales.com

Tasco makes a full line of good-quality, reasonably priced rifle scopes. The optics are brilliant, but many of these scopes won't stand up to heavy recoil from large-bore, centerfire rifles. Exposure to excessive moisture may cause problems. Some scopes are fragile, but the company usually will repair damage free of charge. Sales are through dealers and distributors.

Thompson Target Technology
618 Roslyn Ave. SW
Canton, OH 44710
www.cantorweb.com/thompson targets

This company makes a wide variety of innovative targets for both the bull's-eye shooter and the hunter.

Williams Gun Sight Co.
7389 Lapeer Rd.
Davison, MI 48423

Williams is a long-established company that makes quality sights and scope mounts for the 10/22 rifle.

Winchester Ammunition
427 N. Shamrock St.
East Alton, IL 62024
www.winchester.com

Winchester makes a full line of rimfire ammunition. Perhaps the most useful is Winchester Dynapoint, available through K-Marts across the United States.

ABOUT THE
AUTHOR

Mark White has been making, modifying, and working on firearms for more than 50 years. He is a graduate of the State University of New York at Buffalo, with both a bachelor's degree and a master of science degree in industrial education. He spent the 1970s and 1980s working at the University of Alaska as a college professor. Over the past four decades, his magazine articles devoted to the Ruger 10/22 rifle have made him the nation's foremost authority on this weapon. His company, Sound Technology, located in Pelham, Alabama, is a leader in the field of sound suppression for firearms. He is shown here with his very first 10/22. It is called The Chameleon because of all the changes, variations, and barrels it has gone through over the years. Photo by Al Paulson